Lillian C. Buttre

The American Portrait Gallery

With biographical sketches of presidents, statesmen, military and naval heroes,

clergymen, authors, poets, etc. - Vol. 2

Lillian C. Buttre

The American Portrait Gallery
With biographical sketches of presidents, statesmen, military and naval heroes, clergymen, authors, poets, etc. - Vol. 2

ISBN/EAN: 9783337194109

Printed in Europe, USA, Canada, Australia, Japan

Cover: Foto ©Thomas Meinert / pixelio.de

More available books at **www.hansebooks.com**

THE
AMERICAN
PORTRAIT GALLERY.

WITH

BIOGRAPHICAL SKETCHES

OF

PRESIDENTS, STATESMEN, MILITARY AND NAVAL HEROES, CLERGYMEN, AUTHORS, POETS, Etc., Etc.

BY

LILLIAN C. BUTTRE.

STEEL PLATE ILLUSTRATIONS.

NEW YORK:
J. C. BUTTRE, PUBLISHER,
48 FRANKLIN STREET.

Entered according to Act of Congress, in the year 1877, by
J. C. BUTTRE
In the Office of the Librarian of Congress at Washington, D. C.

Trow's
Printing and Bookbinding Co.,
Printers and Bookbinders,
205-213 East 12th St.,
New York.

PREFACE.

Few works of fiction offer anything so attractive as the records of past ages, and of the events of the present epoch. But while studying and admiring our general national history, our attention is directed to individual history, or biography, upon which the interest of the whole depends.

As History involves the consideration of Biography, brief biographical sketches, in turn, excite a desire to know more of the characters and their relation to history. The two branches are indeed intimately connected, and greatly dependent upon each other. Biography is, in fact, "History teaching by example." To the force and efficacy of example, Biography adds the weight of precept. It improves our understanding, and enlarges our stores of useful knowledge; bringing to our assistance the experience of others by presenting to our minds a picture of their projects and achievements; of their manners, pursuits, attainments, and mode of thinking; and thus, not only gratifies our curiosity, but teaches us wisdom, and suggests a variety of interesting reflections.

It is the object of this work to convey useful information illustrative of the lives of those whose portraits appear within its pages; and in each sketch to give the most important incidents in the career of its subject. In so condensed a compilation much of interest is of necessity omitted. But in a general and authentic outline, with a few words of personal description, may be found enough to distinctly characterize each individual. The dates, it is believed, are accurate. The same may be said of the allusions to leading events. The entire collection will be found reliable for reference by the reader of the present, and of the future.

CONTENTS.

Vol. II.

1. LINCOLN, ABRAHAM.
2. HOPKINS, EZEK.
3. ADAMS, WILLIAM.
4. GALLAUDET, THOMAS H.
5. SCOTT, WINFIELD.
6. COOPER, PETER.
7. CLARK, THOMAS M.
8. DUYCKINCK, EVERT A.
9. EWING, THOMAS.
10. MITCHEL, ORMSBY McK.
11. BROWNLOW, WILLIAM G.
12. TUCKERMAN, HENRY T.
13. BLAIR, FRANCIS P., JR.
14. MANSFIELD, JOSEPH K. F.
15. CARTWRIGHT, PETER.
16. MORSE, SAMUEL F. B.
17. BUCHANAN, JAMES.
18. HITCHCOCK, ETHAN A.
19. PRATT, ZADOC.
20. POE, EDGAR ALLAN.
21. STOCKTON, ROBERT F.
22. SPRING, GARDINER.
23. STORY, JOSEPH.
24. WEED, THURLOW.
25. JOHNSON, REVERDY.
26. CUSTER, GEORGE A.
27. STORRS, RICHARD S.
28. CUSHING, CALEB.
29. CONKLING, ROSCOE.
30. HALLECK, HENRY W.
31. CHOATE, RUFUS.
32. DE SOTO, FERNANDO.
33. JERVIS, JOHN B.
34. STRINGHAM, SILAS H.
35. SCOTT, THOMAS A.
36. SARGENT, EPES.
37. SEYMOUR, HORATIO.
38. HEINTZELMAN, S. P.
39. NOTT, ELIPHALET.
40. JAY, JOHN.
41. STEUBEN, F. W. VON.
42. DOUGLAS, STEPHEN A.
43. BETHUNE, GEORGE W.
44. WINTHROP, THEODORE.
45. WEST, BENJAMIN.
46. TANEY, ROGER B.
47. WAYLAND, FRANCIS.
48. GAINES, EDMUND P.
49. PIERREPONT, EDWARDS.
50. HUNTER, DAVID.
51. DEEMS, CHARLES F.
52. MORTON, OLIVER P.
53. LITTLEJOHN, ABRAM N.
54. DAVIS, CHARLES H.
55. HASTINGS, S. C.
56. HAYES, RUTHERFORD B.
57. OSGOOD, SAMUEL.
58. GRANT, ULYSSES S.
59. BRYANT, WILLIAM C.
60. ANTHONY, HENRY B.
61. TAYLOR, BAYARD.
62. BONNER, ROBERT.
63. SUMMERFIELD, JOHN.
64. STUYVESANT, PETER.
65. VANDERBILT, CORNELIUS.
66. CALHOUN, JOHN C.
67. JACKSON, ANDREW.
68. HAMLIN, HANNIBAL.
69. BUELL, JAMES.
70. DIX, JOHN A.
71. TYNG, STEPHEN H., JR.
72. SCHURZ, CARL.
73. SEWARD, WILLIAM H.
74. HANCOCK, WINFIELD S.
75. WALL, GARRET D.
76. COKE, THOMAS.
77. SHIELDS, JAMES.
78. CARPENTER, MATTHEW H.
79. EDWARDS, JONATHAN.
80. GOODRICH, SAMUEL G.

ABRAHAM LINCOLN.

"The two great men by whose words and example our glorious Continental Republic is to be fashioned and shaped are Washington and Lincoln: representative men of the East and of the West, of the Revolutionary era and the era of Liberty for all."

Abraham Lincoln, the sixteenth President of the United States, was born in Hardin County, Kentucky, February 12, 1809. When he was in his eighth year the family removed from Kentucky to Spencer County, Indiana. A few months of the rudest sort of schooling comprehended the whole of his technical education; but throughout his life he was constantly adding, by reading and observation, to his stock of knowledge.

In his youth he was in turn a farm laborer, a workman in a saw-mill, and a boatman on the Wabash and Mississippi rivers. Thus hard work and plenty of it, the rugged experiences of aspiring poverty, education born of the log-cabin, the rifle, the axe, and the plough, combined with the reflections of an original and vigorous mind eager in the pursuit of knowledge by every available means, developed a character equally remarkable for resource and firmness. In 1830, Lincoln and his family removed to Decatur, Illinois. In 1832 he volunteered for the Black Hawk War, was elected captain of his company, and served through a three months' campaign. After his return he was an unsuccessful candidate for the Legislature. He then kept store for a short time; was postmaster and surveyor; studying law, meantime.

In 1834 Mr. Lincoln again became a candidate for the Legislature, and was elected. In 1846 he was chosen to the Thirteenth Congress, and served to the close of the session; after which he measurably withdrew from politics and devoted himself to the practice of his profession until the Nebraska Bill of 1854 called him again into the political arena. In 1858 he was a candidate for the United States Senate, in opposition to Stephen A. Douglas. They canvassed the State together. Mr. Lincoln's logic, wit, eloquence, and thorough good nature were alike conspicuous; but Mr. Douglas was elected. In 1860 Mr. Lincoln delivered his celebrated "Cooper Institute Address."

In June of the same year, Mr. Lincoln received the nomination of the Republican party for President; and in the following November was elected. His inauguration took place on the 4th of March, 1861. Throughout the campaign the South had threatened to secede if he were elected. Prominent men both North and South still hoped that war might be averted, but the new Confederate government was rapidly making preparations for the issue. The first gun of the war was fired at half-past four on Friday morning, April 12, 1861. President Lincoln met the crisis calmly and firmly, and throughout the conflict continued to act with equal decision and wisdom.

On the 22d of September, 1862, his "Emancipation Proclamation" was issued, to take effect on the first of the ensuing January.

President Lincoln's second inaugural address, March 4, 1865, "was a remarkable expression of his personal feelings, his modesty and equanimity, his humble reliance on a Superior Power for light and guidance in the path of duty. 'With malice toward none,' was his memorable language, 'with charity for all, with firmness in the right as God gives us to see the right, let us strive on to finish the work we are in; to bind up the nation's wounds, to care for him who shall have borne the battle and for his widow and orphans, to do all which may achieve and cherish a just and lasting peace among ourselves, and with all nations.'"

Hardly had the four years' struggle been brought to a close, when, on April 14, 1865, President Lincoln was shot by an assassin, while seated in a box at a theatre in Washington. The most prominent men of the nation watched sorrowfully by his bedside, waiting in vain for some sign of returning consciousness until the next morning, when he expired.

The funeral was on the 19th inst. It was a day of mourning throughout the entire country. The body, which had been embalmed, was removed to his former home at Springfield, Illinois. The procession may be said to have extended the entire distance. Churches, the principal buildings, private dwellings, and even the engines and cars were everywhere draped in black—every face bore traces of profound sorrow, and almost every citizen wore a badge of mourning.

Abraham Lincoln was a tall, spare man, and over six feet in height. His hair was dark, his eyes expressive, his mouth large and firm. His manners were cordial and genial. "No one approached him without being impressed with his kindly, frank nature, his clear good sense, and his transparent truthfulness and integrity."

ESEK HOPKINS.

AMID the December snows of 1620, the Pilgrim Fathers arrived on the shores of Cape Cod Bay, in the ship "May Flower," and planted a colony where the town of Plymouth now stands. This little band of suffering pioneers were the ancestors of many of our best liberty-loving men. Descended from one of the name, numbered with the company who came in the "May Flower," was Esek Hopkins. He was the son of William Hopkins, a thorough farmer, whose father, Thomas Hopkins, was one of the first to follow Roger Williams to Rhode Island. Stephen Hopkins, an older brother of Esek, was for several years Governor of that colony, and, next to Dr. Franklin, was the oldest member of the Continental Congress who signed the Declaration of Independence. At the breaking out of the Revolutionary War, Esek Hopkins was commissioned Brigadier-General by Governor Cooke, December 22, 1775, and also received a commission from Congress as Commander-in-Chief of the Naval Forces of the country, and was styled Commodore, and sometimes Admiral, in the newspapers of that period. In the winter of 1775-6, Commodore Hopkins repaired to the Delaware, and in February, 1776, put to sea with the first squadron sent out by the colonies, consisting of four ships and three sloops. The fleet sailed from Delaware Bay for the south, by order of Congress, to check the depredations made by vessels sent out by Lord Dunmore, then Governor of Virginia. He proceeded to the vicinity of the Bahama Islands, and made an attack on New Providence. He effected a landing of eight hundred men, captured the forts, seized eighty cannon, and a large quantity of ordnance, stores, and ammunition, which he shipped and carried away. He also took the Governor, the Lieutenant-Governor, and one of the Council prisoners, and sailed for home. On the return voyage, when off Block Island, Commodore Hopkins took the British schooner "Hawke," and the bomb brig "Bolton." They were armed vessels—the former carrying six, and the latter eight guns —which had annoyed the coasters and small craft belonging to Americans. For this act the president of Congress complimented him officially. Two days afterwards he attacked the "Glasgow," of twenty-nine guns, a British sloop-of-war, but suffered her to escape.

Captain Hopkins continued in public office only a short time after this cruise. In June, 1776, he was ordered by Congress to appear before the Naval Committee to reply to charges which had been preferred against him for not annoying the enemy's ships on the southern coast, of having exceeded his instructions in the attack on New Providence, and for want of proper efforts, or courage, for failing to capture the "Glasgow." After a debate, in which he was ably defended by John Adams, he was acquitted, though Congress censured him for not proceeding direct to the Carolinas. Hopkins was directed to resume the command of the fleet and cruise against the British fishery at Newfoundland. But unavoidable delays in getting the ships ready afforded another occasion for the complaints of his enemies. Their efforts ultimately prevailed, in spite of the exertions of Adams, and on the 2d of January, 1778, he was dismissed the service. John Paul Jones says, in a letter written to Mr. Hopkins shortly after the first trial: " I know you will not suspect me of flattery when I affirm I have not experienced a more sincere pleasure, for a long time past, than the account I have had of your having gained your cause at Philadelphia, in spite of party. . . . You will be thrice welcome to your native land and to your nearest concerns. After your late shock, they will see you as gold from the fire, of more worth and value, and slander will learn to keep silence when Admiral Hopkins is mentioned."

Esek Hopkins exerted great political influence in Rhode Island throughout his life, and was often elected to the General Assembly of the State. His burial-place, as well as place of decease, was at North Providence. His gravestone, which exhibits the usual neglected appearance of old rural cemeteries, bears this inscription :

" This stone is consecrated to the memory of Esek Hopkins, Esquire, who departed this life on the 26th day of February, A.D. 1802. He was born in the year 1718, at Scituate, in the State [Rhode Island], and during our Revolutionary War was appointed Admiral, and Commander-in-Chief of the Naval Forces of the United States. He was afterwards a member of our State Legislature, and was no less distinguished for his deliberation than for his valor. As he lived highly respected, so he died deeply regretted by his country and his friends, at the advanced age of 83 years and 10 months.

"' Look next on greatness,—say where greatness lies.' "

W. Adams

WILLIAM ADAMS, D.D., LL.D.

FEW men have possessed more rigid and conscientious integrity than John Adams, LL.D., and few educators have been as distinguished in the training of youth who were afterward eminent in the various spheres of active and professional life. He descended from the old stock of Henry Adams, which has given two Presidents to the United States. His wife, Elizabeth (Ripley) Adams, was a lineal descendant of Governor Bradford, of the "May Flower."

Their son, William Adams, D.D., LL.D., was born in Colchester, Connecticut, January 25, 1807. His parents removed in his infancy to Andover, Massachusetts, where his father became the principal of Phillips Academy. His early education was received at this academy, from which he entered Yale College, New Haven, and graduated in 1827. His theological studies were pursued in the Theological Seminary at Andover. He was licensed to preach in Boston, by the Suffolk South Association, in the spring of 1830. Immediately after leaving the Seminary, in September, 1830, he was invited to the pastorate of the Congregational Church in Brighton, Massachusetts, where he was ordained and installed in February, 1831. Leaving that place, because of the ill-health of his wife, he was invited to become the pastor of the Broome Street Church, in the city of New York, in the summer of 1834. Accepting this invitation, he was installed over the church in November, 1834, by the Third Presbytery of New York.

A large part of this congregation, who thought it advisable to remove to the upper part of the city, withdrew with Dr. Adams in 1853, and erected an elegant church edifice on the corner of Madison Avenue and Twenty-fourth Street, and became known as the Madison Square Presbyterian Church. The building fronts Madison Square and the Fifth Avenue Hotel, and all its surroundings are remarkably elegant. It was erected at a cost of one hundred and seventy-five thousand dollars, all contributed by voluntary subscriptions. The dedication took place in December, 1854.

WILLIAM ADAMS, D.D., LL.D.

Dr. Adams has occupied a very prominent position in the Presbyterian Church from the time he entered the ministry, and has received from the church many marks of its appreciation of his abilities and vital piety. He was Moderator of the New School General Assembly which met in the city of Washington in 1852, and was active in promoting the reunion between the Old and New School Churches in 1870-71. He received the honorary degree of S.T.D., in 1842, from the University of the City of New York, and of LL.D. from the College of New Jersey, at Princeton, in 1869.

The writings of Dr. Adams are highly valued by the Christian community, alike for the perfection of their style and the ability with which the important themes to which they relate are treated. Among his works may be named, "The Three Gardens—Eden, Gethsemane, and Paradise," "Thanksgiving; Memories of the Day, and Helps to the Habit," and "Conversations of Jesus Christ with Representative Men." His sermons are all able, and show his high theological as well as literary culture. All are grand in conception and eloquent in expression.

Dr. Adams is a tall, erect, finely proportioned man, hale and vigorous. He has regular, well-defined features, and a cheerful, intellectual face. His eyes are bright and penetrating, his mouth is expressive of much decision of character, and his brow displays not only physical symmetry, but the evidence of mental superiority. To this striking and attractive presence are added manners at once polished and fascinating. His voice is melodious and adequate to fill the largest building. His tall, erect figure imparts additional impressiveness to his delivery and gesticulation. He is equally happy as an extemporaneous speaker, possessing as he does remarkable fluency, and the command of chaste, effective language.

The pastoral relations of Dr. Adams are probably as agreeable as those of any man in the ministry. He is admired and beloved by his people, and is sincerely attached to them.

They belong to the educated class of society, and he has the pleasure of knowing that his learned efforts in the pulpit are not wasted upon unappreciative intellects. His church is always crowded, and there is no want of religious zeal. Such is the position occupied by Dr. Adams in his denomination, and with the public at large. His influence is at all times commanding and extended, and his position in the church and the community is that of a representative of the highest religious, moral, and intellectual power.

Yours Sincerely,
T. H. Gallaudet

THOMAS HOPKINS GALLAUDET.

It was the rare good fortune of Thomas Hopkins Gallaudet to achieve a great and permanent work of beneficence in the institution of the "American Asylum for the Deaf and Dumb;" to receive the most touching evidences of the filial respect and affection he had inspired, and to have erected to his memory an appropriate and enduring monument of the grateful appreciation of those whom he had benefited on the spot which had previously been the scene of his labors, and of their happiness.

Mr. Gallaudet was born in the city of Philadelphia, December 10, 1787. His father, Peter W. Gallaudet, was of Huguenot descent. His mother was a Hopkins, and descended from one of the first settlers of Hartford, Connecticut. He acquired a good academic education in his native city, and soon after his parents removed to Hartford. In 1802 he entered the Sophomore class of Yale College. There he was graduated in 1805, and commenced the study of law. The profession had few charms for him, and was abandoned when he was appointed tutor in Yale College, in 1808. His health requiring a more active life, he soon after engaged in commercial business. But neither law nor commerce seemed congenial to his taste; and in the meanwhile, having received deep religious convictions, he felt called to the Gospel ministry. He entered the Andover Theological Seminary in 1811, completed his studies there in 1814, and was licensed to preach. Again diverted from a chosen pursuit, he was led by Providence to a field of useful labor far beyond that to which he had aspired.

He was ready for his mission! That mission was the long-neglected field of deaf-mute instruction. While a student at Andover, his attention had been drawn to little Alice Cogswell, a deaf-mute, whose father's residence was in the immediate neighborhood of his own home, and who was also the companion of his own younger brothers and sisters. He succeeded in arresting her attention by his use of signs —the natural language of the deaf and dumb—following it up by such lessons as his own ingenuity could suggest, and with such lights as he could gather from a publication by the Abbé Sicard, which Dr. Cogswell had procured from Paris. Mr. Gallaudet's first experiments proving so successful, Dr. Cogswell felt an irrepressible desire to extend the blessings of his instruction to others similarly afflicted. An association of gentlemen was formed for that purpose; and in 1815 Mr. Gallaudet visited Europe for the sake of qualifying himself to become a teacher of the deaf and dumb in this country. The selfishness and jealousy of the managers of such institutions in England prevented his learning much that was new or useful there; but at the Royal Institution in Paris, under the care of the Abbé Sicard, every facility was afforded him. He returned in 1816, accompanied by Mr. Laurent Clerc, a highly educated deaf-mute, one of the ablest pupils of Sicard, and one of the best teachers in the Paris Institution.

Measures had been taken, in the meanwhile, to found a public institution; and on the 15th of April, 1817, the first Asylum for the Deaf and Dumb established in America was opened, with a class of seven pupils, under the charge of Mr. Gallaudet. It prospered astonishingly, and he lived to see, as the result of his labors, more than a thousand persons receive the benefits of instruction, as well as to witness the establishment of other institutions for deaf-mutes in different parts of the country. Mr. Gallaudet was married, on the 10th of June, 1821, to Miss Sophia Fowler, of Guilford, a deaf-mute, with whom his acquaintance commenced while she was a member of the first class of pupils instructed by him at the asylum.

He resigned the office of principal of the Deaf and Dumb Asylum, in 1830, although he never ceased to take an active interest, as director, in its affairs. He published many public addresses and contributions to periodicals, and several works designed for educational purposes. He was among the most earnest advocates of the entire subject of female education, and of the employment of women as teachers; was early interested in the establishment of the "Hartford Female Seminary," and delivered an address in its behalf in 1827, which was subsequently published. Wherever a field of Christian philanthropy called for a laborer, there he was found a willing worker.

On the 6th of June, 1838, Mr. Gallaudet became connected, as chaplain, with the "Connecticut Retreat for the Insane," at Hartford, the duties of which office he continued to discharge with exemplary fidelity and most happy results to the day of his last illness. He died at Hartford, on the 10th of September, 1851.

WINFIELD SCOTT.

The "Hero of a Hundred Fights" was born near Petersburgh, Virginia, June 13, 1786. He was educated at the Richmond High School, whence he went to William and Mary College, where he studied law. He was admitted to the bar in 1806, and the next year removed to South Carolina. When the Army Enlargement Bill was passed by Congress, he entered the army as Captain of Light Artillery.

In 1809 Captain Scott was ordered to join the army in Louisiana, commanded by General Wilkinson. The next year he was court-martialled and suspended from the army for one year for openly expressing the opinion that General Wilkinson was implicated in Burr's conspiracy. In July, 1812, he was made a Lieutenant-Colonel in the Second Artillery; and in March, 1814, was made a Brigadier-General. In July of that year he decided the battle of Chippewa by a brilliant bayonet charge. For his gallant conduct in this, and the battle of Lundy's Lane, where he was severely wounded, he was brevetted Major-General, presented with a gold medal by Congress, and offered the post of Secretary of War, which he declined.

With the hope of recovering from the effect of his wounds, General Scott travelled for some time in Europe, returning in 1816. In 1836 he conducted the Seminole campaign, which was "well devised, and prosecuted with energy, steadiness, and ability." In 1838 he was ordered to the Canada frontier, and it was mainly through his exertions that war with Great Britain was averted. Upon the death of Major-General Macomb, in June, 1841, he became Commander-in-Chief of the Army of the United States. War was declared with Mexico in May, 1846, and in March, 1847, he invested Vera Cruz, which surrendered after a short siege. Thence to Mexico was a continued series of glorious victories. Cerro Gordo, Jalapa, La Perote, Puebla, Contreras, Cherubusco, Chapultepec, and Melinòs del Rey, fell successively into his hands. When, on the 14th of September, 1847, the second conqueror of Mexico entered "the Halls of the Montezumas," his triumph was complete, and he stood before the world, the most successful general of the age.

WINFIELD SCOTT.

Peace was concluded February 2, 1848, and shortly afterwards General Scott was court-martialled upon charges preferred against him by brevet Major-General Worth. No decision was given, and he eventually resumed his position as Commander-in-Chief of the Army of the United States.

The Whig National Convention, which met at Baltimore in June, 1852, chose General Scott as their candidate for the office of President of the United States. He was defeated by General Pierce, the Democratic nominee.

In 1859 Congress conferred upon the Hero of the War with Mexico an honor which had been previously rendered to no one, save Washington. He was created Lieutenant-General of the Army of the United States, to take rank from 1847, the close of his services in Mexico. The brevet was purposely so framed as not to survive him, and thus became the more clearly a personal distinction.

Soon after the commencement of hostilities in 1861, the old veteran, pressed by the infirmities of age, and feeling himself inadequate to the laborious duties of another campaign, retired from the army. This act elicited, from President Lincoln, the following order, which was read to General Scott at his residence, by the President in person, attended by all the members of his Cabinet:

"On the 1st day of November, A. D. 1861, upon his own application to the President of the United States, brevet Lieutenant-General Winfield Scott is ordered to be placed, and hereby is placed upon the list of retired officers of the Army of the United States, without reduction in his current pay, subsistence, or allowance.

"The American people will hear with sadness and deep emotion that General Scott has withdrawn from the active control of the Army; while the President and unanimous Cabinet express their own and the nation's sympathy in his personal affliction, and their profound sense of the important public services rendered by him to his country during his long and brilliant career; among which will be gratefully distinguished his faithful devotion to the Constitution, the Union, and the Flag, when assailed by paricidal rebellion. ABRAHAM LINCOLN."

Eight days later, General Scott sailed from New York for Europe, to recruit his health. He died at West Point, on the Hudson, May 29, 1866. His latter days were devoted to his "Autobiography," in two volumes, which was published in 1864. He was also the author of "General Regulations for the Army," and of "Infantry Tactics."

PETER COOPER.

Peter Cooper, the well-known American manufacturer, inventor, and philanthropist, was born in the city of New York, February 12, 1791. His maternal grandfather, John Campbell, was an alderman of New York, and Deputy Quartermaster during the Revolutionary War. His father was an officer in the patriot army, who, after the close of the war, established a hat manufactory. Peter commenced in early boyhood to assist his father, and remained in this business until he could make every part of a hat. The family was large, and it was only by great anxiety and hard labor that they were provided for. Peter's schooling consisted of an attendance of half of each day for a single year.

When in his seventeenth year he was placed with John Woodward, to learn the coach-making trade. During his apprenticeship he made for his employer a machine for mortising the hubs of carriages, which proved very profitable to him. When he became of age, his employer offered to build him a shop and set him up in business, but he declined the offer. He next engaged in the manufacture of patent machines for shearing cloth. The business was very successful for a time, but after the War of 1812, lost its value. He then turned to the manufacture of cabinet-ware, and afterwards went into the grocery business in New York, in which he continued three years.

Soon after, Mr. Cooper purchased a glue factory, on a lease of twenty-one years, and engaged in the manufacture of glue, oil, whiting, prepared chalk, and isinglass to the end of the lease. He then bought ground in Brooklyn where the business was continued. In 1828 he purchased three thousand acres of land within the city limits of Baltimore, and on a part of the property, erected the Canton Iron Works. Disposing of it after a while, he bought an iron factory in the city of New York, and turned it into a rolling-mill for rolling iron and making wire. He ran it for several years, and while there first successfully applied anthracite to the puddling of iron. While in Baltimore, he built, in 1830 after his own designs, the first locomotive engine on this continent. In 1845 Mr. Cooper removed the machinery to Trenton, New Jersey, where he erected the largest rolling-mill at that time in the United States, for the manufacture of railroad iron. These works are very extensive, and now include mines, blast-furnaces, and water-power, and are carried on by the Cooper family. In one of these mills the wrought-iron beams for fire-proof buildings were first rolled.

Mr. Cooper took great interest and invested large capital in the extension of the electric telegraph. He was the first and only president of the New York, Newfoundland, and London Telegraph Company, which continued its operations for eighteen years. He was honorary director of the Atlantic Telegraph Company, president of the American Telegraph Company, and president of the North American Telegraph Association, which at one time represented more than two-thirds of all the lines in the United States. He took an active part in the laying of the Atlantic cable, and early interested himself in the New York State Canals.

Mr. Cooper has served in both branches of the New York Common Council, and was a prominent advocate of the construction of the Croton Aqueduct. He was a trustee in the Public School Society, and when it was merged in the Board of Education, he became a School Commissioner. He felt that no common school system, nor the academy and college could supply the technical knowledge and practical education needed by the industrial classes. He had felt the want of education in his own youth, and the establishment of an institution where free instruction might be obtained became his favorite project.

In 1854 he laid the corner-stone of the large building known as the "Cooper Institute," "to be devoted forever to the union of art and science in their application to the useful purposes of life." It is situated at the junction of the Third and Fourth Avenues, and their crossing with Eighth Street, in the centre of the industrial and trading population of New York City. The institution has a school of art for women, taught in the daytime, in which free instruction is given in all branches of drawing, in painting, wood-engraving, and photography. It has also a free school of telegraphy for young women. In the evening the free schools of science and art for young men and women are opened. There is, besides, a large free reading-room and library, where access may be had to all the periodicals and papers, foreign and domestic, and to over ten thousand volumes.

Thomas M. Clark.

THOMAS MARCH CLARK.

Thomas M. Clark, D.D., Bishop of the Protestant Episcopal Church in the State of Rhode Island, was born in Newburyport, Massachusetts, on the 4th of July, 1812. After graduating at Yale College in 1831, he studied theology at Princeton, New Jersey, and was licensed to preach by the Presbytery in 1835. He had charge for a short time of the Old South Church in Boston; but having resolved to enter the Episcopal Church, he was ordained in January, 1836, and became rector of Grace Church, Boston, where he remained until 1843, when he removed to Philadelphia. He resided in that city for the next four years. At the end of that time he returned to Boston and became assistant minister of Trinity Church. In 1851 he was rector of Christ's Church in Hartford, Connecticut. Elected Bishop of Rhode Island, he was consecrated on the 6th of December, 1854, in Grace Church, Providence, of which parish he was rector for twelve years.

Bishop Clark has published numerous charges and addresses, and is the author of "Lectures on the Formation of Character," "Purity, a Source of Strength," "The Efficient Sunday-School Teacher," "An Efficient Ministry," "Early Discipline and Culture," and "Primary Truths of Religion." The last-named work has been translated into the Chinese language for the use of schools in China and Japan. It is admirably adapted to meet the unsettled condition of mind which prevails so extensively in these days in regard to the fundamental principles of morals and religion. Not only in this country, but in Europe, this timely treatise has been received with unqualified favor. The *Allgemeine Literarische Zeitung*, of Berlin, thus characterizes it: "We find in this book of the Bishop of Rhode Island a contribution to Christian apologetics of great interest and value. The book discusses, in five parts, the problems of Theism, the fundamental principles of morals, revelation, inspiration, and Christianity. The great questions pertaining to these several heads, Bishop Clark has most satisfactorily solved with a genuine philosophical spirit, and on the basis of comprehensive studies. The work gives evidence throughout of the author's familiarity with the fundamental problems of the philosophy of religion. The Bishop is, without doubt, an eloquent and original thinker, and his work, which in its logical development is acute, clear, and precise, will enchain the interest of the readers for whom it was written. As a short but exhaustive book for doubters, we greet this production of one of the most distinguished members of the American Episcopate, and wish for it an abiding success."

A few of the concluding paragraphs will serve as an illustration of the Bishop's clear and forcible reasoning and his simple and eloquent diction. In speaking of the position of Jesus Christ in history, after referring to the degenerated condition of Palestine and the untoward circumstances of our Saviour's childhood in respect of instruction in spiritual or divine knowledge, he proceeds: "Out of this dull background the full-formed figure of Jesus suddenly flashes into light. There is no visible preparation for His great work—no pupilage, no study, no discipline, no earthly antecedent to account for the phenomenon—the ideal man, He for whose advent the world had been waiting through weary centuries, suddenly appears, moves about Galilee and Judea for a few months, and then vanishes from the scene. But, during this short space, He has said something, He has done something, which has made the world another place to what it was before, and man another being to what he was before; even the face of eternity is changed, and the grave itself has become radiant—His name has become a talisman—the slave hears it and leaps his chains; the sinner hears it and ceases from his sin; the weary and heavy-laden hear it and find rest; the dying saint hears it and falls asleep in Jesus.

"It will not be questioned that no human being has ever improved the world like Jesus of Nazareth. The quiet words that He uttered, as He sat with a little group of disciples on some Galilean hill-side, have been taken on the wings of the wind and carried to every quarter of the earth. What He said and did and endured soon found its chroniclers, and this record has become the sacred Book of the most civilized of modern nations and has received the extraordinary title of 'The Word of God.'"

Evert A. Duyckinck.

EVERT AUGUSTUS DUYCKINCK.

The name of "Duyckinck" appears among the earliest Dutch annals of the city of New York. Christopher Duyckinck took an active part on the popular side in Revolutionary times. His son, Evert, was a leading publisher during the first quarter of the present century.

Evert Augustus Duyckinck, son of Evert, was born in the city of New York, November 23, 1816. He was educated at Columbia College, graduating in 1835. He studied law in the office of John Anthon, and was admitted to the bar in 1837. His tastes and associations inclined him to a literary life. After an extended tour in Europe he returned to New York, and in December, 1840, commenced, with Cornelius Matthews, a new monthly periodical, entitled "Arcturus, a Journal of Books and Opinion," which was continued through three volumes, closing in May, 1842. To this work he contributed essays, articles on old English authors, and reviews.

Mr. Duyckinck, in the early part of 1847, entered upon the editorship of "The Literary World," a new weekly review of books, the fine arts, etc., which, with the exception of an interval of about a year, during which the work was conducted by Charles Fenno Hoffman, was carried on to the close of 1853. Mr. Duyckinck had the aid of his talented younger brother, George Long Duyckinck, in the editorship. At the close of this publication, Mr. Duyckinck and his brother were again united in a work to which their familiarity with the authors of the day formed a useful preparation. "The Cyclopedia of American Literature," projected by the late Charles Scribner, was committed to their hands, and for about two years exclusively occupied their attention. The first edition appeared in 1856, and ten years afterwards a "Supplement" was added by its senior editor. To the merits of this standard work, it can be scarcely necessary here to allude. The discriminating and courteous tone in which it truthfully narrates and illustrates the progress of our literature, is a happy medium between the laudatory and the censorious extremes of criticism.

Mr. Duyckinck, in 1856, edited a volume entitled "Wit and Wisdom of the Reverend Sydney Smith, being Selections from his Writings, and Passages of his Letters and Table Talk, with a Biographical Memoir and Notes," a work which passed through several editions. In 1862 he wrote the letter-press to the "National Portrait Gallery of Eminent Americans," issued by Messrs. Johnson, Fry & Co., New York, in two volumes, quarto, a series of Biographies, from the Revolutionary era to the present day, of which over a hundred thousand copies have been issued. He also edited a contemporary "History of the War for the Union," in three quarto volumes; a "History of the World," in four volumes, mainly arranged from the "Encyclopedia Britannica," and an extensive series of Biographies of "Eminent Men and Women of Europe and America," in two volumes, quarto, all for the same publishers.

Among other miscellaneous literary productions, Mr. Duyckinck edited, with a memoir and notes, "Poems Relating to the American Revolution, by Philip Freneau," New York, 1865; and the American edition of "Poets of the Nineteenth Century." He was also the author of a "Memorial of John Allan," an eminent New York book collector, printed by the Bradford Club in 1864; and Memorials of Francis L. Hawks, D.D., Henry Theodore Tuckerman, John David Wolfe, and James William Beekman, were read before the New York Historical Society, and printed for that institution.

For the last forty years of his life Mr. Duyckinck resided at No. 20 Clinton Place, New York City, where he died on the 13th of August, 1878. He left a widow, but no surviving children. His house was always the resort of the most eminent literary men. He had one of the choicest libraries in the State, and he may be said to have lived among his books. Those who knew him intimately, speak of him as a genial and interesting companion, of singularly sweet disposition, and with a soul as little soiled by the world as can be possible to humanity. His memory will be treasured by many of his associates who survive him, and an enduring monument of his scholarly taste and research will exist in his library, enshrined as it is intended to be, in Mr. Lenox's noble repository of works of literature and art. There can be no memorial more fitting for the quiet and genial man of letters, whose name, honorably identified with the growth of his native city and with its best culture, will thus be linked with all that is most permanent and elevating in the works of human genius.

THOMAS EWING.

THOMAS EWING, LL.D., an eminent lawyer and statesman, was born near West Liberty, Ohio County, Virginia, on the 28th of December, 1789. George Ewing, his father, was born in Greenwich, New Jersey, where the family lived before the Revolution. He was present at the battles of Germantown and Brandywine, and spent the winter of 1777 at Valley Forge. His pecuniary resources were considerably diminished by the exigencies of the times, and at its close he removed with his family to Virginia, and afterwards to Ohio, where he settled upon a small tract of land on Federal Creek, in Athens County. The spot selected was then in the wilderness, and seventeen miles beyond the frontier settlements. For nearly three years the family were shut out from all intercourse with the world. Here young Ewing grew up, taking his full share of the hard work and rough experiences of the frontier life of that day. He received his early education chiefly from an elder sister. When about nineteen years of age he set out for the Kanawha salt mines, to work on his own account. For the next few years his life was one of alternate toil and study. In 1815 he was graduated from the University of Ohio, receiving the first degree of A.B. ever issued by that institution. Fourteen months more of diligent study of the law completed his prescribed course, and in August, 1816, he was admitted to the bar. His rise was rapid. His reputation and practice increased with each succeeding year.

In 1830 Mr. Ewing was elected to the Senate of the United States by the Legislature of Ohio, and took his seat in the following year. He found Webster, Clay, Calhoun, Benton, Preston, Wright, and other leading spirits of the nation, in the Senate. A Whig in politics, he co-operated with Clay and Webster in opposition to the policy of Jackson. One of his first speeches was made in opposition to the confirmation of Martin Van Buren as Minister to England. He was a warm supporter of the protective tariff policy of Clay, advocated a reduction of the rates of postage, a re-charter of the National Bank, and the rev enue collection bill, known as the Force Bill. Among the prominent measures with which he was identified was his bill for reorganizing the Post-Office Department, which passed the Senate without a division on the 9th of February, 1835, though it was lost in the House. He introduced a bill for the settlement of the Ohio boundary question, which passed in 1836, and was the author of the act for reorganizing the General Land Office.

At the expiration of his senatorial term in 1837, Mr. Ewing resumed the practice of law. In 1841, President Harrison appointed him Secretary of the Treasury, and he continued in office for a short time under Tyler. When Taylor became President in 1849 he appointed him Secretary of the new Department of the Interior, which was as yet unorganized. He resigned the office when Fillmore succeeded Taylor to the Presidency in July, 1850. He was then appointed to a seat in the Senate, to fill a vacancy caused by the resignation of Governor Corwin, who went into Mr. Fillmore's Cabinet. During this term, which expired in March, 1851, he refused to vote for the Fugitive Slave Law, helped to defeat Mr. Clay's Compromise Bill, presented a petition for the abolition of slavery in the District of Columbia, and asked that it might be appropriately referred, at the same time expressing himself opposed to the granting of the prayer of the memorialists. Mr. Ewing then retired once more to the practice of his profession, in which he continued throughout the remainder of his life, though for the last few years he only attended to a small number of cases.

Mr. Ewing was a delegate to the "Peace Congress" of 1861. Though not taking an active part in the late Civil War, he closely watched its progress, and was deeply interested in the result. He was an earnest supporter of President Lincoln and of the National Government. For several years he was regarded as one of the leading Whig politicians of Ohio. In his last days he acted with the Democratic party. He died at Lancaster, Ohio, on the 26th of October, 1871.

"In person, Mr. Ewing was large and stoutly built, so that he was physically as well as intellectually a strong man. In his early hard labor in felling the forests of the West, and in feeding the furnace of the salt works, his figure must have been developed and strengthened much more than if in early life he had been devoted wholly to sedentary pursuits; and at the same time he was confirmed in habits of industry that he never lost." In manner quiet, self-controlled, gentle, and courteous; always exhibiting one of the most endearing marks of true greatness—kindness and consideration for youth.

ORMSBY McKNIGHT MITCHEL.

MAJOR-GENERAL O. M. MITCHEL was a native of Kentucky, having been born in Union County, in that State, on the 28th of August, 1810. When he was two years old the family removed to Lebanon, Ohio, where he received his early education. He was appointed a cadet at the West Point Military Academy in 1825, and on graduating, July 1, 1829, received the commission of Second Lieutenant in the Second Regiment of Artillery. The following month he was appointed Acting Assistant Professor of Mathematics at West Point, which position he retained until August, 1831.

Mitchel resigned his military rank in 1832, began the study of law, was admitted to the bar in Cincinnati, Ohio, and practised two years. From 1834 to 1844 he held the position of Professor of Mathematics, Philosophy and Astronomy in Cincinnati College. From 1836 to 1837 he was Chief Engineer of the Little Miami Railroad, and in 1841 was one of the Board of Visitors to West Point Military Academy. He became the founder and director of the Cincinnati Observatory in 1845, and retained the latter position for several years, during which time he edited and published the "Sidereal Messenger," an astronomical journal. In 1847 he was appointed Adjutant-General of Ohio, and in 1848 Chief Engineer of the Ohio and Mississippi Railroad. During the same year he published a series of ten lectures in a volume entitled "The Planetary and Stellar Worlds." In 1858, when the troubles in the Dudley Observatory left it without a manager, Professor Mitchel was called to the vacant post. He was very popular as an astronomical lecturer, and perfected instruments for recording right ascensions and declinations by electro-magnetic aid, and for the accurate measurement of large differences of declination. He was the author of "A Treatise on Algebra," "Astronomy of the Bible," and the "Orbs of Heaven." Such is the brief history of this gallant General before the war.

At the great meeting at Union Square, New York, Prof. Mitchel was one of the principal speakers, and his oration was unequalled for patriotic fervor and splendid imagery. His devotion to the Union was not unheeded, for on August 9, 1861, the President appointed him a Brigadier-General in the volunteer force of the United States from New York. He was ordered to the Department of the Ohio, where he engineered the series of fortifications around Cincinnati that checked the audacious march of Kirby Smith upon that city. His command rapidly increased from a brigade to a division, and then to a column. He took Cynthiana, and then, in rapid succession, seized every other point on the railroads reaching to Lexington and Frankfort, and controlling the entire north and centre of the State.

In February, 1862, he occupied Bowling Green, after a forced march of forty miles over almost impassable roads, in twenty-eight hours. Astonished at his appearance, Buckner fled precipitately, leaving the "Gibraltar of Kentucky," with its immense accumulation of military stores, to fall into the hands of the Federal troops.

After the occupation of Nashville, he made a forced march southward, seized the railroad between Corinth and Chattanooga, captured Huntsville, and occupied various points in northern Alabama. On the 15th of October, 1862, the President recognized his valuable services by appointing him a Major-General in the volunteer service of the United States. In September, General Mitchel was withdrawn from the field, and after weeks of weary waiting was given the command of the Department of the South, with headquarters at Beaufort. He at once commenced reorganizing the forces, and, with his usual industry and perseverance, had nearly completed preparations for a projected campaign, when he was seized with yellow fever, and, after a brief illness, died at Beaufort, South Carolina, October 30, 1862.

General Mitchel was well described by the Reverend Henry Norman Hudson, an army chaplain at Hilton Head. "In person he is rather spare, in stature rather short, with a head capacious, finely shaped and firmly set, an attractive and beaming countenance, every feature and every motion full of intelligence and animation. Therewithal, he is a man of keen discernment and large discourse; swift-thoughted, fluent, and eloquent of speech, free and genial in his dispositions, quick and firm of purpose, of clear and intense perceptions, and sound and steady judgment. All who have met him in the lecture-room must have admired the enthusiasm and whole-souledness of the man in whatever he does or says. Yet a strong force of judiciousness goes hand in hand with his enthusiasm. He is indeed brilliant, but not flashing; his brilliancy is that of a solid, not of a surface."

WILLIAM G. BROWNLOW.

On the 29th of August, 1805, William Gannaway Brownlow was born in Wythe County, Virginia. He was left an orphan in early childhood, and was reared by his mother's relatives, who appear to have been persons of slender means, as the boy was early accustomed to hard labor and received only sufficient education to enable him to read. He led a life of labor and drudgery until he attained his eighteenth year, when he launched into life on his own account. Removing to Lynchburg he apprenticed himself to a house carpenter, and regularly learned the trade, finding time, however, for improving his mind; and his first earnings were devoted to obtaining additional schooling.

It is related of him that, while attending a protracted Methodist camp-meeting, the religious exercises affected him so profoundly that he felt "called upon to preach the Gospel." Having been duly ordained in 1821, he entered the Methodist ministry, and for ten years went from place to place preaching the Gospel. His sermons were noted more for their vigor than their elegance. As early as 1828 he began to take part in politics in Tennessee, advocating the re-election of John Quincy Adams to the Presidency. While travelling a circuit in South Carolina, in which John C. Calhoun lived, he took part in the nullification controversy, opposed the project, and in consequence of the strong opposition excited against him, published a pamphlet in his own vindication.

About 1837 he became editor and proprietor of a celebrated and widely circulated political newspaper—the "Knoxville Whig." In connection with this paper, and in consequence of his trenchant mode of expression, he obtained the *sobriquet* of "the fighting parson."

In reply to attacks made upon the Methodist Church, he published in 1856, a work entitled "The Iron Wheel Examined, and its Spokes Extracted." In 1859 he held a public debate in Philadelphia with the Reverend A. Pryne, of New York, which was published in a volume entitled "Ought American Slavery to be Perpetuated?" Mr. Brownlow taking the affirmative.

From the beginning of the secession movement in 1860, he boldly advocated in his paper the principle of adherence to the Union, as the best safeguard of Southern institutions. This course subjected him to much persecution after the secession of Tennessee.

Until the 24th of October, 1861, Parson Brownlow, as he was universally called, continued the publication of the "Whig" at Knoxville. Subsequently remaining for some time concealed, he was induced, by a promise of passports, to report to the commanding General at Knoxville, where he was arrested in December, 1861, on a charge of treason against the Confederacy, and detained until March, 1862, when he was released, and escorted to the Union lines at Nashville. On his arrival in the Northern States Mr. Brownlow made a tour of the principal cities, speaking to large audiences in behalf of the Union cause. Upon the reoccupation of Knoxville by the Northern forces, he returned to that city, previously announcing his purpose to revive his paper, and with funds supplied by his sympathizers at the North he resumed his editorial duties.

Shortly before the war ended Mr. Brownlow was elected Governor of Tennessee by the loyal voters of the State, and remained in that office from 1865 to 1869, when he was elected to the Senate of the United States.

When Mr. Brownlow took his seat in the Senate he was suffering greatly from physical depression. He took the oath of office, and then sank back in his cushioned seat, exhausted by the effort. The few votes that he cast during the session were partisan. Almost his last appearance in the political arena was the support of Mr. Senter, the Conservative candidate for Governor of Tennessee. This action and the result of the election contributed greatly to restore Tennessee to peace and tranquillity.

Mr. Brownlow died at Knoxville, Tennessee, April 29, 1877.

Honest, straightforward, and fearless, the stern, unbending patriotism of the man vailed all his minor faults.

In person Mr. Brownlow was slender, about the medium height, with long arms and hands, was sallow complexioned, and had high cheekbones. His style of speaking was deliberate, though rough. It was thoroughly ad captandum. His personal habits were singularly pure; he never tasted liquor, never used tobacco, never had seen a theatrical performance, and never dealt a pack of cards—a remarkable record.

HENRY THEODORE TUCKERMAN.

HENRY THEODORE TUCKERMAN is a descendant of an ancient English family of that name. He was born in Boston, Massachusetts, April 20, 1813. In 1833, after preparing for college, the state of his health rendered it necessary for him to abandon study for a time and spend a few months in the milder climate of Europe. Upon his return, he resumed his studies, and in 1837 again visited Europe. In 1845 he removed from Boston to New York, and from that time the last-named city was his home. In 1850 he received the honorary degree of Master of Arts from Harvard University. In the winter of 1852 he spent a few weeks in London and Paris.

Mr. Tuckerman has a wide reputation as an elegant writer and discriminating critic. His writings include poems, travels, biographies, and essays. "A characteristic of his books is that each represents some phrase or era of experience or study. Though mainly composed of facts, or chapters which in the first instance appeared in the periodical literature of the country, they have none of them an occasional or unfinished air. They are the studies of a scholar—of a man true to his convictions and the laws of art. His mind is essentially philosophical and historical; he perceives truth in its relation to individual character, and he takes little pleasure in the view of facts unless in their connection with a permanent whole. Hence what his writings lose in immediate effect, they gain on an after-perusal. His productions pass readily from the review or magazine to the book."

The published works of Mr. Tuckerman are, "The Italian Sketch Book;" "Isabel, or Sicily, a Pilgrimage;" "A Month in England;" "Thoughts on the Poets," the first of his collections from magazines. This was followed by "Artist Life, or Sketches of American Painters," a classical volume, which added to the author's already enviable reputation. His materials were drawn, in several instances, from facts communicated by the artists themselves. "The sketches are written with a keen appreciation of the unworldly, romantic, ideal life of the artist. Picturesque points are eagerly embraced. There is a delicate affection for the theme which adapts itself to each artist and his art." "A Memorial of Horatio Greenough," prefixed to a selection from the sculptor's writings, was published several years later. "Characteristics of Literature, illustrated by the Genius of Distinguished Men," in two series of papers, was published in 1849 and 1851. In 1850 "The Optimist; a Series of Essays," appeared. "Leaves from the Diary of a Dreamer" was published in 1853. In 1851 a collection of his poems was published, the principal of which is the "Spirit of Poetry." In 1851 he published "Essays, Biographical and Critical, or Studies of Character." In this volume, which contains nearly five hundred pages, there are thirty separate articles. Washington Irving wrote: "I do not know when I have read any work more uniformly rich, full, and well sustained. The liberal, generous, catholic spirit in which it is written is beyond all praise. The work is a model of its kind." In 1859 his "Character and Portraits of Washington" was published. Two years later, soon after the commencement of the Civil War, he published "The Rebellion; its Latent Causes and True Significance." "The essay is written in a patriotic spirit, with firmness and candor, and will remain a thoughtful memorial of the times, to be consulted by the philosophical historian." "A Sheaf of Verse Bound for the Fair" was contributed to the great fair of the Sanitary Commission, held in 1864 in New York City. The same year he published an elaborate work, entitled "America and her Commentators, with a Critical Sketch of Travel in the United States." In 1866 "The Criterion; or, The Test of Talk about Familiar Things," appeared. The year after, "The Maga Papers, About Paris," were reprinted. In 1868 was issued "Book of the Artists: American Artist Life; Comprising Biographical and Critical Sketches of American Artists, preceded by an Historical Account of the Rise and Progress of Art in America, with an Appendix, containing an account of Notable Pictures and Private Collections." This is in many respects the substantial crowning effort of the author's literary career. "The Life of John Pendleton Kennedy," published in 1871, was his last work. He has also been a contributor to the best magazine literature of the day.

Mr. Tuckerman died in New York City on December 17, 1871. "He was literally in the midst of his busy literary avocations when the summons came. He may be said almost to have died with the pen in his hand."

FRANCIS PRESTON BLAIR, JR.

GENERAL FRANK P. BLAIR, JR., was born in Lexington, Kentucky, February 19, 1821. His father, Francis Preston Blair, a prominent politician, was for several years the editor of the "Globe," a Democratic journal, published in Washington. Montgomery Blair — an elder brother of F. P. Blair, Jr. — is a well-known politician. He was graduated at West Point, in 1835, and served in the Seminole war. He practised law in St. Louis, and in 1839 was appointed United States District Attorney for Missouri; was Judge of the Court of Common Pleas, and, later, Solicitor of the United States in the Court of Claims. In 1861, President Lincoln appointed him Postmaster-General, which post he held for three years.

Frank Blair, Jr., was educated at Princeton College, from which he was graduated in 1841, at the age of twenty. While still a very young man, he emigrated to Missouri, and settled in St. Louis, where he studied law, and was admitted to the bar. There he early became prominent in politics, under the leadership of Mr. Benton. In 1845, he made a journey to the Rocky Mountains for his health, and was in New Mexico when the war between the United States and Mexico broke out. He joined the command of Kearny and Doniphan, and served as a private soldier until 1847, when he returned to St. Louis, and resumed the practice of his profession.

In 1848, Mr. Blair attached himself to the Free Soil party, and, from this time forward, opposed the extension of slavery into the Territories, both as a public speaker and in the "Missouri Democrat," of which he was the editor for a time. In 1852, and again in 1854, he was elected a member of the Missouri Legislature, from St. Louis County. He was elected a representative to the Thirty-fifth Congress, in 1856, and was a member of the Committee on Private Land Claims. He was re-elected in 1858 and in 1860, and was Chairman of the Committee on Military Affairs. In 1857 he delivered an elaborate speech in the House of Representatives, in favor of colonizing the black population of the United States in Central America.

The suggestion did not find favor at the South, but received the sanction of Lincoln and other prominent politicians. His last term in the House of Representatives was finished in 1862, but he did not wait for its close to begin his military career.

As early as February, 1861, Mr. Blair enrolled a regiment in St. Louis, and succeeded in keeping his secret until its services were required in the field. He was the first man to enroll himself as a private in the regiment, but was afterwards elected colonel. On the 7th of August, 1862, he was appointed Brigadier-General, and November 29th of the same year he was appointed Major-General of Volunteers, and immediately afterwards set out for the Army of the West, then under the command of General Grant. About this time Grant's forces were divided, and General Blair's Brigade was attached to General Sherman's corps. He took part in the unsuccessful assault upon Vicksburg, and in the movements against Arkansas Post, which opened the way to Little Rock and the interior of the State. In the subsequent operations against Vicksburg, under Grant, General Blair succeeded Sherman in the command of the Second Grand Division in the Fifteenth Corps, and in October was appointed by Sherman commander of the corps. After the capitulation of Vicksburg General Blair joined in the active pursuit of General J. E. Johnston's forces, and in the attack upon and final capture of Jackson, Mississippi. Under General Sherman he took part in the advance of the forces from the Mississippi River toward Chattanooga, and in the battles before that city on the last of November, 1863. As he had, however, been elected during the fall of 1862 to represent the First District of Missouri in Congress, the Government appointed General Logan to relieve him of his command, that he might take his seat. The President soon after nominated him anew Major-General of Volunteers, and he again served under Sherman, and was in the advance guard of the march from Atlanta to the sea.

In 1866 General Blair was appointed Collector of Customs in St. Louis, and Commissioner of the Pacific Railroad. For some years he had acted with the Republican party, but, becoming dissatisfied, he returned to the Democratic party, and, in 1868, became the candidate of that party for the office of Vice-President. In 1870, he was chosen United States Senator from Missouri, the term expiring in March, 1873. Political disappointments subsequently superinduced a paralytic stroke. For more than two years he lingered a helpless invalid. His death occurred in St. Louis, Missouri, July 8, 1875.

JOSEPH KING FENNO MANSFIELD.

The ancestors of General Mansfield were of English extraction, and were among the most distinguished of the early American colonists. Joseph K. F. Mansfield was the youngest child of Mary F. and Henry S. Mansfield, and was born at New Haven, Connecticut, December 22, 1803. Before he reached the age of fourteen he received a cadet's appointment and entered the Military Academy at West Point, where he early gave promise of future greatness. He was graduated with high honors in 1822, the youngest in years, and the second in rank in his class. Receiving a commission in the corps of Engineers, he became a brevet Second Lieutenant. In this position he continued for nearly ten years, his commission as First Lieutenant bearing date March, 1832.

From 1826 to 1828 he acted as Assistant Engineer, in the construction of Fort Hamilton, at the Narrows, in New York Harbor. For the next two years he was similarly engaged in the building of Fortresses Monroe and Calhoun, at Old Point Comfort. Fort Pulaski, at the mouth of the Savannah River, is a monument of his labors and genius as an architect. For these and many other high professional services Lieutenant Mansfield became a Captain of Engineers in 1838.

Throughout the Mexican War, he was Chief Engineer of the army commanded by General Taylor, and possessed his fullest respect and confidence. Arriving at Point Isabel, General Taylor ordered Mansfield to plan its defence. In half a day the ground was surveyed, the key to the position determined, a redoubt traced to cover it, and he joined his commander at Matamoras, when he was ordered to erect a battery to command the town and construct a fort to hold the position. The main army now fell back on Point Isabel. With his garrison weak, his works unfinished, his materials to be brought from miles away, he must show that he could not only build forts, but defend them. The storm soon came. Threatened in rear by light troops, bombarded in front by heavy batteries, the devoted garrison fought and labored, and the army, as it came, shattered and bleeding, but victorious, from the plains of Palo Alto and Resaca de la Palma, saw the loved flag of the Union still flying defiant over the little garrison of Fort Brown. For his distinguished conduct in its defence during a bombardment of a week, Captain Mansfield was brevetted a Major.

The next advance of the army was on Monterey, where, on the second day, Major Mansfield was ordered to make a forced reconnoissance of the enemy's redoubt on the left, and take it if possible. The order was executed and the redoubt triumphantly carried. Early in the battle he was shot through the leg, but he still kept at his work all that day and part of the next, when his wounds compelled him to leave the field, prostrating him for six weeks. He was subsequently rewarded by being appointed Lieutenant-Colonel. The battle of Buena Vista found him again ready for action. This conflict began February 22, 1847, and lasted two days. For his services and gallantry Mansfield was promoted to the rank of Colonel.

At the close of the war Colonel Mansfield was assigned to duty at the fortifications of Boston Harbor, became a member of the Board of Engineers, and in 1853 was appointed Inspector-General of the Army. In this distinguished capacity he inspected the Department of New Mexico once, and California and Texas twice, and had just returned from the latter field when he was appointed, on the 14th of May, 1861, Brigadier-General in the Regular Army of the United States, and was summoned to the defence of Washington. He fortified the city on every side, crowned the Heights of Arlington, and took Alexandria. By his iron will, sleepless energy, constant industry, and untiring courtesies to all under and around him in those perilous hours, he entitled himself to the gratitude and honor of his country.

General Mansfield was afterwards placed successively in command of Forts Monroe, Hatteras, Camp Hamilton, and Newport News, at which latter place he saved the "Congress" from the sad fate of the "Cumberland," when the "Merrimac" assailed those mighty ships of war in the most signal battle recorded in naval history. During Pope's campaign, and in the second battle of Bull Run, he was in active service. At his own request, after the invasion of Maryland, he was ordered to report to General McClellan, and was assigned to the head of the corps previously under the command of General Banks. At Antietam, September 17, 1862, he was mortally wounded.

General Mansfield was a man of fine appearance and of exalted private character. As a soldier he was brave, fearless, and a strict disciplinarian. He was one of the most celebrated of our generals, and had few equals as a scientific engineer.

PETER CARTWRIGHT.

Peter Cartwright, one of the pioneers of Methodism in the West, was born September 1, 1785, in Amherst County, on the James River, Virginia. His parents were poor. His father served over two years in the Revolutionary War, and after independence was declared, moved to Kentucky, which was then an almost unbroken wilderness, abounding in valuable game of various kinds. The early settlers suffered many hardships while clearing the country and preparing to cultivate the fertile soil. They were constantly annoyed by the surrounding hostile Indian tribes, all of whom regarded Kentucky as a common hunting-ground. Soon after the settlements were established travelling ministers commenced going the rounds of the country, preaching as they went. Among the foremost and most active were the Methodist brethren.

As young Peter Cartwright grew from childhood to boyhood, and from boyhood to young manhood, the population in the vicinity of his home increased rapidly; the country improved, and the people began to enjoy many of the privileges of civilized life. Still, at the best, they lacked many comforts and even necessaries. There were few schools and few churches, as the preaching was almost entirely done by the itinerancy. Mrs. Cartwright was a devoted member of the Methodist Episcopal Church, and often entertained the ministers of that denomination at her home. In 1801, when Peter was in his seventeenth year, he joined the same church. Before his conversion, as he said many years later in life, he caused his mother the greatest anxiety by his devotion to horse-racing, card-playing, dancing, and company. He was a most successful gambler. All these habits and amusements were abandoned when he joined the church.

In the spring of the next year, before he had reached the age of seventeen, he received, much to his surprise, a license " to exercise his gifts as an exhorter in the Methodist Episcopal Church." In the autumn of that year the family moved to a new home near the mouth of the Cumberland River. Previous to this time Peter had received but little education, but shortly after they were settled in their new abode he entered a school a few miles distant, where the English branches and the dead languages were taught. He soon became deeply interested in his studies, and was progressing rapidly when he was unfortunately compelled to leave the school in consequence of the persecution of some of his fellow-students.

In the spring of 1803 young Cartwright started out to form a circuit (it was afterward called Lexington Circuit), holding meetings and organizing classes as he journeyed from place to place. In the fall, soon after he had passed his eighteenth birthday, he preached his first sermon.

In 1806 Mr. Cartwright was elected and ordained deacon of the Methodist Episcopal Church, by Bishop Asbury, and in 1808 elder, by Bishop M'Kendree. In 1812 he was appointed a presiding elder. He was a member of every quadrennial conference from 1816 to 1860, and again in 1868. The first annual conference he attended was held in 1803 and for a great many years afterward he rarely missed one of these meetings. He travelled eleven circuits and twelve presiding elders' districts. During his ministrations he received ten thousand persons into the Methodist Church on probation and by letter, and baptized over twelve thousand adults and children.

When Mr. Cartwright commenced his career as an itinerant, an unmarried preacher was only allowed eighty dollars per annum. But they seldom received over thirty or forty dollars, and often much less. Some idea of their experiences may be gained from Mr. Cartwright's own description. "We sat on stools or benches for chairs, ate on puncheon tables, had forked sticks and pocket or butcher knives for knives and forks, slept on skins before the fire, or sometimes on the ground in the open air, had our saddles or saddle-bags for pillows, and one new suit of clothes of homespun was ample clothing for one year, for an early Methodist preacher in the West. We crossed creeks and large rivers without bridges or ferry-boats, often swam them on horseback, or crossed on trees that had fallen over the streams, drove our horses over, and often waded out waist deep; and if by chance we got a dug-out or canoe to cross in ourselves, and swim our horses by, it was quite a treat."

Mr. Cartwright died near Pleasant Plains, Sangamon County, Illinois, September 25, 1872. He was the author of "Fifty Years a Presiding Elder," and of "The Autobiography of Peter Cartwright, the Backwoods Preacher."

SAMUEL FINLEY BREESE MORSE.

The distinguished American artist who invented the Electric Telegraph was the eldest son of Reverend Jedediah Morse, of Connecticut, the first writer on geography in this country. He was born in Charlestown, Massachusetts, April 27, 1791. Samuel Finley, his mother's grandfather, was President of the College of New Jersey.

Young Samuel Morse, after receiving a thorough elementary education, studied at Yale College, where he was graduated in 1810. While a student there he paid special attention to the study of chemistry and natural philosophy, which he pursued under the instruction of Professors Silliman and Day. His predilection for science was strong, but he had also as decided a liking for art. The latter prevailed, and the year after his graduation he sailed for Europe under the care of Washington Allston. Upon his arrival in London he made the acquaintance of a talented young painter — Charles R. Leslie. Benjamin West evinced a deep interest in the success of the youthful artists, and gave them much valuable instruction. So industrious was Mr. Morse that after two years of study and practice he exhibited at the Royal Academy in London his famous picture, "The Dying Hercules." The model of the figure, which he first formed, won the prize of a gold medal from the London Society of Arts. The next year he painted the "Judgment of Jupiter," a picture highly praised by West. In 1815 he returned to the United States. After a short stay in Boston, Mr. Morse went to New Hampshire, and for a time painted portraits at fifteen dollars each. He next went to Charleston, South Carolina, where his talents were appreciated, and his prospects much improved. In 1822 he took up his residence in New York City. Under the auspices of the City Corporation, he painted a full-length portrait of La Fayette. In the autumn of 1825 Mr. Morse was instrumental in forming an Association of Artists — a "Society for Improvement in Drawing" — from which grew the National Academy of Design. He became the first President of the institution, and delivered a course of lectures on the Fine Arts.

In 1829 Mr. Morse again visited Europe, and was absent three years. While abroad the position of President of the Literature of the Arts in the New York University was offered him, and he returned home. On the voyage an incident occurred which resulted in his invention of the Telegraph. "He embarked in the autumn of 1832, at Havre, on board the packet ship 'Sully,' and through a casual conversation with some of the passengers, on the recent discovery in France of the means of obtaining the electric spark from the magnet, showing the identity or relation of electricity and magnetism, Morse's mind conceived not only the idea of an electric telegraph, but of an electro-magnetic and chemical recording telegraph, substantially and essentially as it now exists."

Professor Morse commenced the construction of the apparatus he had sketched within three months after his arrival at home. In 1835 he demonstrated the practicability of his plan in the New York University, by putting a model telegraph in operation. In the course of two or three years it had progressed so far that Mr. Morse petitioned Congress for an appropriation to erect a Telegraph line from Baltimore to Washington. After several discouraging postponements, $30,000 were placed at his disposal. In 1844 the work was completed.

"The subsequent history of the inventor and the invention reveals further trouble—vexatious lawsuits for the infringement of the patent, as well as the establishment in the courts of the right thereto, and the difficulty there was in persuading capitalists to aid in constructing other lines. But after these obstacles had been overcome, Professor Morse reaped the reward of his noble labors. His name was covered with honor in every civilized country. The diplomatic representatives of ten nations combined to vote him 400,000 francs as a collective testimonial. The Sultan of Turkey presented the Order of Nishan Iftichar set in diamonds; the King of Prussia bestowed gold medals in a solid gold snuff-box; Denmark, Austria, Wurtemberg, France, and Spain honored him with decorations. Banquets and receptions were tendered him in many of the chief cities of the world; a statue has been erected to him in Central Park, New York. He lived to see the fruit of his thought applied in every country of the Eastern Continent, and in the Western fifty thousand miles of land traversed by telegraphic wires. He was a welcome and honored guest wherever he appeared."

Professor Morse died at his residence in New York, April 2, 1872, at the age of eighty-one.

JAMES BUCHANAN.

The fifteenth President of the United States was born at Stony Batter, Franklin County, Pennsylvania, on the 22d of April, 1791. When but eighteen years of age he was graduated from Dickinson College with the highest honors of his class. He immediately began the study of law, and was admitted to the bar in 1812. He rose rapidly in his profession, and by the time he had reached the age of thirty it was generally admitted that he stood at the head of the bar in his native State. His practice was both extensive and lucrative, and his success was such that he was enabled to retire with a competency when but forty years of age.

In 1814, Mr. Buchanan first entered the public service of his country. In that year he was elected to the Pennsylvania Legislature by the Federalists. In 1820, he took his seat in Congress, and by successive re-elections remained a member of the House of Representatives for ten years. He supported General Jackson for the Presidency in 1828. In 1831, he received the appointment of American Minister to Russia. On his return in 1833 he was elected by the Pennsylvania Legislature to a seat in the United States Senate. His associates there were the leading men of the nation—Webster, Clay, Calhoun, and Wright. He advocated the expunging of the resolution of censure upon President Jackson, whose administration he warmly supported. The financial difficulties, which had been continually multiplying throughout Jackson's administration, reached a crisis soon after Van Buren's accession to the Presidency. Buchanan now warmly advocated the creation of an independent treasury, in opposition to Webster, Clay, and others. This measure was temporarily set aside during the administrations of Harrison and Tyler.

Mr. Buchanan urgently advocated the annexation of Texas, thus again coming into conflict with Clay and Webster. On the Omnibus Bill, or Compromise of 1850, however, he cordially agreed with them, and urged its favorable reception upon the people. During the twelve years he was Senator, he was a recognized leader of the Democracy, and always strongly opposed the agitation of the Slavery question.

He believed that the proper course was "to leave this question where the constitution has left it, to the slaveholding States themselves."

When Polk became President in 1845, he called Buchanan to his cabinet as Secretary of State. At the close of this administration Mr. Buchanan retired to his home in Pennsylvania, where he lived in the comparative seclusion of private life during the four years that Taylor and Fillmore were in office.

Upon the elevation of Pierce to the Presidency, he was appointed Minister to England. The plan of purchasing Cuba now arose. A Conference of the American Ministers to France, Spain, and England met at Ostend. Mr. Buchanan declared that if Cuba could not be purchased from Spain, we should be justified in wresting it from that country rather than endanger the peace of the Union. The Conference issued the "Ostend Manifesto" as the result of their deliberations, and for a time it caused intense excitement in this country and in Europe. He returned to the United States in April, 1856, and in the summer of the same year the Democratic Convention, which met at Cincinnati, nominated him for the Presidency. He was elected, and was inaugurated on the 4th of March, 1857.

Mr. Buchanan was a man of imposing personal appearance, an accomplished gentleman, endowed with superior abilities improved by the most careful culture, and no word had ever been breathed against the purity of his moral character. His long experience as a legislator, and the exalted offices he had held at home and abroad, eminently fitted him for the station he was called to fill. Under ordinary circumstances his administration would probably have been a success.

His avowed purpose was "to destroy any sectional party, whether North or South, and to restore, if possible, that national fraternal feeling between the different States that had existed during the early days of the Republic." But party jealousies and popular feeling were too strong to be easily overcome. Intense excitement on the slavery question prevailed throughout Mr. Buchanan's administration.

Upon the election of Mr. Lincoln the South declared its determination to secede. President Buchanan did not interpose. "He might by a few words have rendered the nation the most signal service; but those words were not spoken." At the expiration of his term he retired to private life. He wrote in 1866 "Mr. Buchanan's Administration," a work explaining and defending his own measures.

The "bachelor President" died at his home near Lancaster, Pennsylvania, June 1, 1868.

ETHAN ALLEN HITCHCOCK.

At the falls on Otter Creek, Vermont, seven miles from Lake Champlain, is the beautifully situated and picturesque little city of Vergennes. There on the 18th of May, 1798, Ethan Allen Hitchcock, the author and military officer, was born. His father was Judge Samuel Hitchcock, and his mother was the daughter of Ethan Allen, who was so prominent in the early history of Vermont.

Young Hitchcock, after preliminary studies, entered the Military Academy at West Point, and graduated in 1817. In 1824 he became assistant instructor in tactics in the same institution, and from 1829 to 1833 was commandant of cadets and instructor in infantry tactics. Previous to 1829, except for three years, he served on garrison and recruiting duty.

At the outbreak of the Florida War, which grew out of an attempt to remove the Seminole Indians to lands west of the Mississippi, in accordance with a treaty, he volunteered his services, and became acting inspector-general in Gaines' campaign of 1836. The little army of which he was a member, not only experienced the hardships of a contest with a cunning and desperate enemy in a strange country, but suffered from want of food at times. He was subsequently transferred to Indian duty, where in his position as disbursing agent, he was valuable in protecting the Indians against swindlers.

During the war with Mexico, Hitchcock served in all of General Scott's battles, and part of the time as inspector-general. For his services in the battles of Contreras and Churubusco he received the brevet of Colonel, and for those rendered in the battle of Molino del Rey he was brevetted Brigadier-General. After the close of the war he crossed the ocean and spent some time in an extended tour through Europe and in the East.

In April, 1851, he was appointed Colonel of the 2d Infantry, and was ordered to San Francisco, California, where he commanded the

ETHAN ALLEN HITCHCOCK.

Military Division of the Pacific. In October, 1855, he resigned his commission in consequence of the refusal of Jefferson Davis, then Secretary of War, to confirm a leave of absence granted by General Scott. He afterward resided at St. Louis, devoting himself mainly to literary pursuits, and to certain philosophical investigations in which he had evinced a thoughtful interest for many years.

On the breaking out of the late civil war, Mr. Hitchcock offered his services to the Government of the United States. On the 10th of February, 1862, he was appointed a Major-General of Volunteers. He was then more than three-score years of age and did not take an active part in the campaign. Still he did not shrink from the share which fell to him in those stirring times. He was placed on duty in the War Department, and to these duties were added, in November, those of Commissioner for the exchange of prisoners of war, and Commissary-General of Prisoners. In December of the same year he was commissioned to revise the military laws and regulations. He discharged the various duties of these offices with ability until October, 1867.

Mr. Hitchcock was an accomplished officer, and had ever been much interested in the prominent public events relating to the welfare of his country. While taking a more or less active part in them he still found time for pursuits more congenial to the taste of the careful student. As the result of his labors he leaves a name among the authors of America as well as a record among her officers.

The first of his works, "The Doctrines of Swedenborg and Spinoza Identified," appeared before the public in 1846. After a silence of eleven years, "Remarks upon Alchemy and the Alchemists" was published in 1857. The succeeding year, 1858, he published "Swedenborg a Hermetic Philosopher." This was followed by a work in two volumes, entitled "Christ the Spirit, being an Attempt to State the Primitive View of Christianity." His other works are, "Red Book of Appin, and other Fairy Tales," "Remarks on the Sonnets of Shakspeare," "Spenser's Colin Clout Explained," and "Notes on the Vita-Nuova of Dante."

Mr. Hitchcock died at Hancock, Georgia, August 5, 1870.

ZADOC PRATT.

The life of this gentleman, for many years one of the most prominent manufacturers and Democratic politicians in the State of New York, was, from the commencement of his career, a checkered one. "It exhibits pointed facts and established truths that should be taught to the rising generation. It tells, in a language that they cannot mistake, that labor, perseverance, probity, and integrity will lead to independence and affluence, and gather honors for its votaries. It will show to them that there is but one road to pursue, and that is the path of virtue; that though thorns may peer at first through its narrow opening, yet the path widens as they advance, and flowers bloom to welcome them."

Mr. Pratt was born at Stephentown, Rensselaer County, New York, October 30, 1790. His father was a tanner, with limited means, who could afford to give his son but little education. At an early age Zadoc began learning the trade of his father, at Middlebury. During his leisure hours, he braided whip-lashes, the sale of which, after a little time, brought him the amount of thirty dollars, a large sum in those days for a boy to earn in addition to the performance of his regular duties. He was next apprenticed to a saddler, and upon the expiration of his time was employed by his father and brothers.

After working for a year as a journeyman saddler, at ten dollars a month, young Pratt commenced business for himself. With an unusually large share of activity and industry, he devoted fifteen or sixteen hours per day to labor. He commenced by keeping an exact account of all business transactions, and continued this systematic course throughout his business life. After a few years spent as a saddler and harness-maker, he sold his store and entered into partnership with his brothers in the tanning business. In 1819 he disposed of his share in the concern, and undertook an adventure for his brothers, to Canada, to traffic in furs.

A few years later, Mr. Pratt again recommenced the business of tanning, in a limited way at first, but finally on a grand scale. Up in the Catskill Mountains he established a gigantic tannery, five hundred and fifty feet long, said to be the largest in the world. In about a score of years during which the business was carried on there, a million of sides of sole leather were tanned, and the quality of the work was as admirable as the quantity was great. For bark and wood alone half a million dollars was paid; and some six millions of dollars expended without a single case of legal litigation.

He founded the settlement of Prattsville village, building over a hundred houses, besides helping to erect an academy and several churches.

In 1823 Mr. Pratt was elected Colonel of the One Hundredth Regiment of New York, and made his own military saddle and bridle, which were handsomely ornamented with silver.

Mr. Pratt entered into politics as an advocate of Democratic principles, and he remained true to the party to the end of his life. In 1836 he was chosen one of the Presidential Electors. The same year he was elected a Representative in Congress for the Eighth Congressional District of New York. He made himself familiar with the duties of his office, and labored successfully for the public good. In 1842 he was re-elected. While in Congress he advocated reduction in the rates of postage; his plans for the Post-Office buildings were adopted; he addressed the House of Representatives for the purpose of having constructed a dry dock at Brooklyn; and was the originator of the Bureau of Statistics. He voted for the first telegraph line from Baltimore to Washington, and advocated the appropriation of ten thousand dollars for surveying the route of a railroad to the Pacific. He held his last official position in 1852, that of a presidential elector. The same year he was a delegate to the Baltimore Convention, and numerous other Democratic conventions. He was president of many societies and institutions. He travelled extensively in his own and foreign countries. His death took place at Bergen, New Jersey, April 6, 1871.

"Over eighty years on earth was vouchsafed to Mr. Pratt. In the long evening of his life, honored and respected for his uprightness and integrity by all who knew him; looked up to with veneration and gratitude by the many whom his counsel or charity befriended, the old tanner of the Catskill Mountains must have looked death fearlessly in the face, conscious that he had done his duty in the flesh and had naught to apprehend and everything to hope for in the world to come."

EDGAR ALLAN POE.

EDGAR ALLAN POE was born in Baltimore, in the early part of the year 1811. The Poe family was one of the oldest and most respected in Maryland. David Poe, the grandfather of the poet, was a distinguished officer of the Maryland line of the Revolutionary Army, and the intimate friend of LaFayette. His son, the father of Edgar A. Poe, was educated for the law, but upon his marriage with an English actress he abandoned his profession and went upon the stage. He and his wife died within a few weeks of each other, leaving three young children entirely destitute. Edgar, who was an unusually bright and beautiful boy, was adopted by a friend of his parents, John Allan, a wealthy merchant of Richmond, Virginia.

In 1816, Mr. and Mrs. Allan took their adopted son to England, and placed him in a school near London, where he remained four or five years. After his return home he studied for a time under private tutors, and then entered the University of Virginia. There he distinguished himself as a scholar and an athlete. At the end of a year, though he took the first honors, he was expelled from the college, and went home greatly in debt. A few years later he entered West Point Military Academy, but after a few months' stay he was court-martialled and expelled from the Academy. Poe once more returned home, and was kindly received by Mr. Allan, who had just married a second time. A quarrel with the young wife, who was many years the junior of her husband, resulted in the final ejectment of Poe from his adopted home. Mr. Allan died shortly afterwards, leaving an infant son heir to his vast estates, and bequeathing nothing to Poe.

Young Poe, brought up in luxury, was now thrown upon his own resources. His education and habits were not such as to fit him for a business life. When other means failed, his taste impelled him to literary pursuits. He had already written a number of poems, which had been published in a volume, at Baltimore, in 1829. In 1833, the proprietor of a weekly literary journal in that city offered two premiums, one for the best prose story, and one for the best poem. Poe sent in two articles, and the examining committee, of whom John P. Kennedy was one, awarded to him both the prizes. Mr. Kennedy subsequently procured him the position of Editor of the "Southern Literary Messenger," in connection with Thomas W. White. He remained in this situation for nearly two years, and was rapidly gaining a high reputation when his irregularities forced the publisher to dismiss him. At one time he had an engagement with every leading magazine in America, but his unfortunate disposition and habits prevented him from retaining such associations for any great length of time.

The best known of Poe's productions is "The Raven," which made him famous. His works in prose and verse are numerous. His poems are characterized by ingenuity, melody, and taste. Among the most remarkable of his works are "The Gold Bug," "The Fall of the House of Usher," "The Murders in the Rue Morgue," "The Purloined Letter," "A Descent into the Maelstrom," and "The Facts in the Case of M. Valdemar."

Poe had an erect and somewhat military bearing. His figure was slight but finely proportioned, and his pale intellectual face was lighted up by remarkably brilliant eyes. He died at a hospital in Baltimore, October 7th, 1849, while on his way to New York to make preparations for his second marriage. A night spent with some of his boon companions resulted in a fit of insanity, from which he died in a day or two.

"It will be difficult to reconcile his wild and reckless life with the neatness and precision of his writings. The same discrepancy was apparent in his personal conduct. Neat to fastidiousness in his dress and in his handwriting, ingenious in the subtle employment of his faculties, with the nice sense of the gentleman in his conduct and intercourse with others while personally before them—there were influences constantly reversing the pure, healthy life these should have represented. Had he been really in earnest, with what a solid brilliancy his writings might have shone forth to the world. With the moral proportioned to the intellectual faculty he would have been in the first rank of critics. In that large part of a critic's perceptions, a knowledge of the mechanism of composition, he has been unsurpassed by any writer in America; but lacking sincerity, his forced and contradictory critical opinions are of little value as authorities, though much may be gathered from them by any one willing to study the mood in which they were written."

Yours truly
R. F. Stockton

ROBERT FIELD STOCKTON.

RICHARD STOCKTON came from England about 1670, and first settled on Long Island, in the colony of New York. Thence he went to New Jersey, and purchasing some seven thousand acres of land near Princeton, in 1682, effected the first European settlement made in that part of the province. There, for many succeeding generations, his descendants have lived and died. His great-grandson was Richard Stockton, a prominent lawyer of Revolutionary times, who was a delegate to the Continental Congress of 1776-7, and a signer of the Declaration of Independence. He was captured by a party of Royalists in 1776, thrown into prison at New York, and treated with great severity. Congress took up his cause, and threatened Lord Howe with retaliation upon British prisoners. This had the desired effect, and he was soon afterwards exchanged; but the enemy had destroyed his library, and devastated his lands. His oldest son, Richard Stockton, LL.D. (father of the subject of our sketch), was a Senator of the United States under the administration of Washington, and subsequently a Member of the House of Representatives. He was eminently distinguished for his talents, was an eloquent and profound lawyer, and during more than a quarter of a century stood at the head of the bar in New Jersey.

Commodore Robert Field Stockton, U. S. N., was born at Morven, the old family-seat, near Princeton, in 1795. Though a promising scholar, he left his books at the age of sixteen, and sought and obtained a commission in the navy. He entered as midshipman, and his conduct in several battles gained him honorable notice. In 1814, when but eighteen years old, he was promoted to a lieutenancy for gallantry in action. The next year, while first lieutenant of the "Spitfire," he distinguished himself by boarding an Algerine war vessel with a single boat's crew.

In 1821, the American Colonization Society placed Stockton in command of the "Alligator" and sent him to the coast of Africa,

The expedition was successful. He obtained, by treaty from the native chiefs, a large and valuable tract of country, and the present Republic of Liberia was founded. He also captured many slavers, and on his return broke up many nests of West India pirates.

In 1838, Stockton was promoted to a captaincy, and visited England as bearer of dispatches. While there he devoted himself to the study of naval architecture. He was one of the first of our commanders to introduce and apply steam to naval purposes. The famous sloop-of-war "Princeton," built according to his designs and under his supervision in 1844, furnished the model for numerous other vessels.

In 1845, Commodore Stockton was sent to the Pacific, and after a voyage of over eight months, his vessel, the "Congress," arrived on the coast of California. With but one thousand five hundred men, including six hundred sailors, he conquered the whole of California in about six months, and established the authority of the United States. The way was thus opened for the annexation of this valuable territory. Through the Commodore's instrumentality the foundations of religion, education, and social progress were laid in many of our Western outposts. Upon his return in 1847 he was greeted with high honors, and received the enthusiastic congratulations of his countrymen. After serving his country in every quarter of the globe for nearly forty years, he now retired to private life.

Commodore Stockton occasionally entered the political arena. He aided internal improvements in his native State, was warmly in favor of General Jackson's administration, and a strong opponent of the election of Martin Van Buren. In 1851 he was elected to the United States Senate, where he expressed his views upon all important questions with frankness and fearlessness. He procured the passage of a law for the abolition of flogging in the navy. In 1853 he resigned his seat in the Senate. He died at his old home near Princeton, October 7, 1866.

"The most prominent and marked characteristic of Commodore Stockton was decision. This was the secret of his success. It enabled him, both in civil and military life, to overcome difficulties which seemed insurmountable. Self-reliance and energy were depicted on his countenance and illustrated in his every movement. He possessed great integrity of character. He was social and genial in his disposition, and domestic in his habits, kind and benevolent to the poor and true to his friends."

GARDINER SPRING.

In the year 1634, John Spring, with his wife Eliza, embarked at Ipswich, England, for America, with their four children. They settled in Watertown, Massachusetts, near Boston, where his name is on the earliest list of proprietors in 1636. Their descendants for succeeding generations were representatives of the best New England type. One of these was the Reverend Samuel Spring, D.D., a leading divine, and one of the chaplains to the portion of the Revolutionary Army that accompanied Arnold in his attack on Quebec in 1775, and who carried Burr, when wounded, off the field in his arms. At the close of the war he became pastor of the church in Newburyport, Massachusetts, and continued in that position till his death. His son, Gardiner Spring, D.D., LL.D., was born there, February 24, 1785. He seemed to have been devoted to the ministry of the Gospel from childhood by his parents. They cherished this purpose long before he accepted it. With this end in view, he was sent, at the age of twelve, to Berwick Academy, in Maine, then celebrated for its thoroughness in classical studies. But the attractions of home were so strong that he was allowed to make his preparation for college mainly in the schools of Newburyport. In the year 1799, at the age of fifteen, he entered as Freshman in Yale College. Excessive application to study impaired his health, and for the year following he pursued his studies in the Academy at Leicester, Massachusetts. Then re-entering college in the class below his former one, he pursued his collegiate studies, and was graduated with the highest honors of his class in 1805. Immediately after his graduation, he began the study of law in the office of Judge Daggett, of New Haven. An opportunity shortly presenting itself to go to the island of Bermuda, as a teacher, and being at that time entirely dependent on his own resources, he accepted it, and remained there some fifteen months. After his return, he completed his law studies in the office of Stephen Smith, then United States Senator, and was admitted to the bar in December, 1808. He began the practice of law with a fair prospect of success, but his attention having been long turned to religious subjects, he spent a year at Andover Theological

Seminary, and toward the end of 1809 was licensed to preach the Gospel.

He soon after received a call to the pastorate of the "Brick Church," and on the 10th of August, 1810, was ordained to the ministry and installed as pastor of that church by the Presbytery of New York.

The "Brick Church" formerly occupied the triangular lot of ground bounded by Park Row, Nassau and Beekman Streets, where the "World," "Times," and other buildings now stand. This lot was obtained from the corporation by the Wall Street Presbyterian Congregation—the first organization of that sect in New York—and a church erected upon it, which was dedicated in January, 1768. During the Revolutionary War the church was used by the British as a prison and hospital for prisoners of war. After the evacuation of New York, the church was repaired and reopened in June, 1784, by its pastor, John Rodgers, D.D. He was the first and only pastor, from its opening in 1768, until 1810, when Dr. Spring was installed. This property was sold by the congregation, after long occupation, for a large sum, and a purchase made of lots on the corner of Fifth Avenue and Thirty-seventh Street, where one of the most magnificent and spacious church edifices of the city was erected. Dr. Spring removed with his people to the new church in 1858, and preached on the 31st of October in that year, the sermon dedicatory of the building. In the pastorate of this church his life was spent, maintaining, during sixty-three years, a distinguished position among the most popular preachers and esteemed divines of the metropolis. He died in New York City, August 18, 1873, in the eighty-ninth year of his age.

Dr. Spring was the author of several works, and made the press the servant of the pulpit, by gathering up the best fruits of his pulpit preparations, and publishing them in a continuous and growing series, which extended to some twenty octavo volumes. Among them are "The Attraction of the Cross;" "The Mercy Seat;" "First Things;" "The Glory of Christ;" "The Power of the Pulpit;" "Short Sermons for the People;" "The Obligations of the World to the Bible;" "The Church in the Wilderness;" "Memoirs of the late Hannah L. Murray;" "Memoirs of the Rev. S. J. Mills;" "Fragments from the Study of a Pastor;" "The Bible not of Man;" "Discourse to Seamen;" "Contrast between Good and Bad Men;" "Brick Church Memorial;" "Pulpit Ministrations;" "Personal Reminiscences," etc. They have passed through several editions, and have been in part reprinted and translated in Europe, and are held in well-deserved repute.

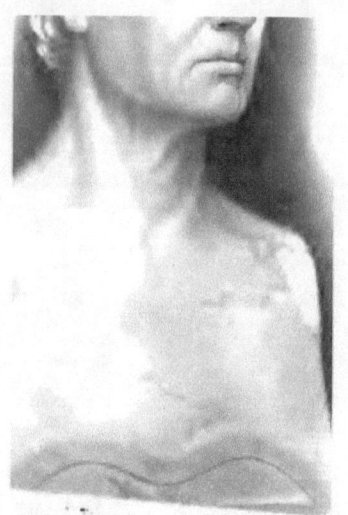

JOSEPH STORY.

This distinguished jurist was born at Marblehead, Massachusetts, on the 18th of September, 1779. His father, Dr. Elisha Story, was a native of Boston, ardent in the cause of liberty, an active participant in the memorable destruction of tea, and afterwards a surgeon in the Army of the Revolution. Subsequently, retiring from the service, he settled at Marblehead, where he practised medicine with success and celebrity.

Joseph Story received his early education in the academy of his native town, then under the superintendence of the Reverend Dr. Harris (afterward president of Columbia College, New York), where he made such rapid progress in learning that he was enabled to enter Harvard University, at Cambridge, in 1795, a half-year in advance, and was graduated there with high and well-earned honors in 1798. On leaving the university, he promptly decided in favor of the profession of law, the study of which he commenced under the Honorable Samuel Sewall, and completed with Judge Samuel Putnam. He was admitted to the bar in 1801, and made Salem his place of residence and professional practice. His high talent was speedily appreciated, and he soon possessed an extensive and lucrative practice. He was often opposed to the most eminent lawyers of the day, who were Federalists, he having become attached to the Democratic party at the commencement of his professional career. In 1805 he was chosen to represent Salem in the Massachusetts Legislature, and was annually re-elected to that station until 1811. In the meanwhile (1808-9) he was elected a Representative in the Federal Congress, to supply the vacancy in Essex South District, occasioned by the death of Mr. Crowninshield. He served only during the remainder of the term for which he was chosen, and declined a re-election. But in that brief space of time, in two important movements, he distinguished himself: one advocating a general increase of the navy, and the other in his efforts to obtain a repeal of the famous Embargo Act.

Mr. Story was only thirty-two years of age when President Madison appointed him one of the Associate Justices of the Supreme Court of the United States. Withdrawing from the political arena, he labored incessantly to become eminently useful as a jurist. He was an able coadjutor of the illustrious Marshall, and in Commercial and Constitutional Law he had no peer on the bench of the Federal Judiciary.

In 1829, a new Professorship of Law having been created in Harvard University, bearing the name of Dane, in honor of its munificent founder, Judge Story was nominated, and accepted the position as its first professor. Upon this occasion he removed his residence from Salem to Cambridge. To the duties of his new office—accepted for the advancement of his favorite science—Judge Story brought the unabated energy and enthusiasm of his early manhood.

Judge Story wrote much and well. In early life he was a writer of poetry. In 1804 he published a volume of poems containing "The Power of Solitude." His judicial works evince extraordinary learning, luminous expositions, and profound views of the science of Law. The most important of his productions are, "Commentaries on the Laws of Bailments;" "Commentaries on the Constitution of the United States;" "Conflict of Laws," treatises on the law of agencies, bills of exchange and promissory notes, partnership, and commentaries on equity jurisprudence and equity pleadings. To the "Encyclopædia Americana," and the "North American Review," he contributed many valuable papers, and he delivered many addresses upon various important subjects. He received the degree of LL.D. from the colleges of Harvard, Brown, and Dartmouth.

Judge Story died at Cambridge, Massachusetts, on the 10th of September, 1845, at the age of sixty-six years. Posterity will describe him in his own glowing but just delineation of a kindred mind: "Whatever subject he touched, was touched with a master's hand and spirit. He employed his eloquence to adorn his learning, and his learning to give solid weight to his eloquence. He was always instructive and interesting, and rarely without producing an instantaneous conviction. A lofty ambition of excellence, that stirring spirit which breathes the breath of heaven and pants for immortality, sustained his genius in its perilous course. He became what he intended, the jurist of the commercial world, and could look back upon a long track illumined with glory." The "Life and Letters of Joseph Story" were published in 1851, by his son, William Wetmore Story, the poet and artist, who has resided since 1848 in Italy, and is especially distinguished as a sculptor.

THURLOW WEED.

Thurlow Weed, the well-known American journalist, was born at Cairo, Greene County, New York, November 15, 1797. He lost his parents early in life, and was thrown upon his own resources. His education was obtained in common schools, to which he may possibly have devoted six months' time in all. He became a cabin boy on a Hudson River sloop when ten years of age, and two years later entered the country printing-office of Machy Croswell, at Catskill, and for the next few years was employed at different newspaper offices in several villages of the interior of New York State. Before he had grown out of his boyhood, he began to regard with interest the political discussions of the times, and, even at that early period, was a stormy advocate of a war with Great Britain. At the commencement of the war, young Weed, now nearly sixteen years of age, volunteered his services, enlisted as a drummer-boy, and served on the northern frontier. He also served as quartermaster-sergeant.

At the close of his short experience of military life, he returned to his trade, and in a short time became an efficient pressman and a fair compositor.

On becoming of age, he established the "Agriculturist," printed at Norwich, Chenango County, New York. During the next few years he edited several other papers. He achieved nothing but debts by his successive attempts at village journalizing — the country being new, readers poor and scattered, and newspapers superabundant. So the year 1824 found him again a journeyman printer, working for seven or eight dollars a week, in Albany, and on this pittance supporting a family. In 1825 he removed to Rochester, and there became editor of a daily paper, at eight dollars per week.

The abduction and presumed death by violence, at the hands of the Freemasons, of William Morgan, of Batavia, took place in 1826-7. Most of the people of Western New York, were deeply excited on the subject, and formed an Anti-Masonic party. Weed became editor of the "Anti-Masonic Enquirer" (its Rochester organ), identifying himself with the party. He was twice elected to the lower house of the State Legislature. His tact as a party manager and his services in 1826 in securing the election of De Witt Clinton as Governor, suggested him as a competent person to oppose the "Albany Regency," a body who had the general management of the Democratic party in New York. At the expiration of his second term in the Legislature, in 1830, he accordingly removed to Albany, and assumed the editorship of the "Albany Evening Journal," a newspaper established in the interest of the Anti-Jackson party.

From 1830 to 1862, although a political leader, first of the Whig and afterward of the Republican party, he declined all political office. He was instrumental in the election of Mr. Seward, of the State of New York, as Governor, in 1838 and 1840, and was prominent in procuring the presidential nominations of General Harrison, in 1836 and 1840, of General Taylor, in 1848, and of General Scott, in 1852. He warmly advocated the election of Fremont, in 1856, and of Lincoln, in 1860, although his influence had in each case been exerted in favor of Mr. Seward. He was an advocate of the energetic prosecution of the war, 1861–5. In November, 1861, he was sent to Europe by President Lincoln in a semi-diplomatic capacity, remaining abroad until June, 1862, and exerting an important influence upon English opinion through his personal relations with leading statesmen. Shortly after his return home, he withdrew from the editorship of the "Evening Journal." In 1865, he became a resident of New York City, where he edited for a time the "Commercial Advertiser." He retired from active journalism in 1868, but continued throughout the administration of President Grant, and especially during the grave constitutional crisis ensuing upon the election of 1876, to exert a powerful influence upon the counsels of his party, and was a frequent contributor to the columns of the political journals.

He has published "Letters from Europe and the West Indies" (Albany, 1866), collected from the "Evening Journal," and has given some interesting chapters of "Reminiscences" in the "Atlantic Monthly" (1870) and in other periodicals. He is understood to be engaged in preparing for the press an autobiography and portions of extensive correspondence, which will doubtless afford valuable materials for the political history of the United States, and especially of the State of New York, during the half century in which (with his friends Seward and Greeley) he was the arbiter of the Whig and Republican policy.

REVERDY JOHNSON.

REVERDY JOHNSON was born in Annapolis, Maryland, May 21, 1796. His father, John Johnson, an eminent lawyer, born in the same city, filled consecutively the positions of Attorney-General, Judge of the Court of Appeals, and Chancellor of Maryland.

At the age of six years, Reverdy Johnson entered the primary department of St. John's College, in Annapolis. He received a substantial education from this institution, in which he remained ten years. He left at the age of sixteen, without graduating, and at once began the study of law with his father, who proved an able instructor. He was admitted to the bar in 1815, and for half a century continued in a successful practice. In 1814 he left his professional studies to enlist in a company of volunteers formed to aid in defending the city of Washington from the British. The company reached the field in time to take part in the battle of Bladensburg, August 24. This brief engagement was his only experience of military life.

In 1817 the young lawyer removed to Baltimore. His first appointment was that of State Attorney, and in 1820 he was appointed Chief Commissioner of Insolvent Debtors, which office he held until 1821, when he was elected to the State Senate. At the next election he was again chosen to that office, but resigned in the second year of the term, preferring to devote his attention exclusively to the law. In addition to his professional and senatorial duties, he reported and edited the seven volumes (from 1820 to 1827) of judicial decisions in the Court of Appeals, Maryland, known as "Harris and Johnson's Reports." Mr. Johnson identified himself with the Whig party, and was active in its service. For some years he declined all office, but in 1845 accepted that of United States Senator. He remained a member of Congress until 1849, when he resigned upon receiving the appointment of Attorney-General of the United States by President Taylor, who had just come into office. Shortly after the death of the President he resigned this position, and for the next ten years he turned his whole attention to his profession, practising chiefly in the Supreme Court of the United States.

Mr. Johnson was a Delegate to the "Peace Congress" of 1861; and he was subsequently elected to the House of Delegates, of Maryland, by the voters of Baltimore County. In 1862 he was again elected a Senator in Congress, from his native State, for the term commencing March, 1863, and ending in 1869. Throughout this period he was, as he ever had been, a firm defender of the interests of the Union. Though well advanced in years, during his entire term he was one of the most faithful and industrious members of the Senate. He served on the Library Committee, upon those on the Judiciary and Foreign Relations, also upon the Special Joint Committee on Reconstruction. He was one of the Senators designated by the Senate to attend the funeral of General Scott, in 1866. The same year he was a Delegate to the Philadelphia "National Union Convention," and took a leading part in its proceedings. In June, 1868, he was nominated by President Johnson to the English mission. The nomination was unanimously confirmed by the Senate. While Minister to England he labored zealously to procure the settlement of the Alabama claims by treaty. He won the admiration of the British Ministry by his able and courageous defense of the rights of his countrymen. Upon his return the following year he went to Washington and, as far as he was able to, resumed his profession and continued to practise up to the time of his death, which occurred in Annapolis, February 10, 1876. It was one of the "sad memories of the Centennial year." He had been called to his native city to argue a case before the State Court of Appeals, and by invitation of Governor Carroll was a guest at the Executive mansion. After dining at five P.M., leaning upon the Governor's arm, he retired to rest himself upon a sofa in the parlor. After a short interval his absence was discovered, and the intelligence brought that the dead body of the veteran lawyer had been found lying upon the stone pavement of the carriage-way leading under the porch of the mansion. It was evident that Mr. Johnson, in passing down the front steps, misled by his defective vision, had fallen and received immediately fatal injuries. He lost the sight of one eye in early life, and in his last years the other became almost useless.

Mr. Johnson was of medium height. His face was grave. He was a personal favorite in public and in private life, his manner being courteous and pleasing. As an able and learned American statesman, jurist, and orator, he has won a lasting reputation.

GEORGE A. CUSTER.

Brevet Major-General George A. Custer, U.S.A., was born in the village of New Rumley, Ohio, December 5, 1839. After studying in the common schools, a friend sent him to West Point, in 1857. With high spirits and an impetuous disposition, he found the restraint of the military academy irksome. The course was passed through, however, and he graduated in 1861, just as the great Civil War broke out. He told of himself, that "in a class of thirty-four members, thirty-three graduated above him."

Upon his graduation, Custer, desirous of a military name and fame, reported for duty at Washington. He was presented to General Scott, who, pleased by the appearance of the young cadet, selected him as the bearer of important papers to General McDowell, at Bull Run. Here he first experienced the excitement of a battle. He was soon after placed on staff duty under General Phil. Kearney, and passed nearly a year on various duties, till the opening of the Peninsula campaign. He went to the Peninsula and was placed on McClellan's staff, where he earned promotion to the rank of captain and additional aide-de-camp. He was engaged at Yorktown, Antietam, and in the raid of General Stoneman, then chief of cavalry to the Army of the Potomac. He next served as aide to Stoneman's successor, General Pleasonton. While serving in this capacity he was promoted, June 29, 1863, a brigadier-general of volunteers. With his cavalry brigade he held the right of the line at Gettysburg.

General Custer commanded a brigade of the cavalry corps in the Richmond campaign, from April to August, 1864. Commanding the 3d division Cavalry Corps under Sheridan, he participated in the famous Shenandoah campaign. He routed the Confederate rear-guard at Falling Waters; at Winchester he captured nine battle-flags, and more prisoners than he had men engaged. He rendered most important service at Fisher's Hill, and received the brevet of major-general for his gallantry at Cedar Creek. He routed General Rosser, October 9, 1864, and at Waynesboro captured the remnant of Early's army. To accomplish this he had pushed on ahead of the leading division, marching through deep mud in the midst of a rain-storm, crossed a swollen river, and finally charging a superior force captured everything. When a brilliant charge was to be made, and a defeated or retreating enemy to be pursued, the arduous task was entrusted to the ever-successful Custer. In the battles of the campaign ending in the surrender of Lee, he commanded a cavalry division, and bore a most important part. He distinguished himself at Dinwiddie Court House, at Five Forks, Sailor Creek, and finally at Appomattox Court House. "As a cavalry genius, par excellence, Custer will undoubtedly take rank in the history of the future. After his great chief, Sheridan, we know of no man who contributed more to the surrender at Appomattox than this same 'boy-general.'" At the age of twenty-six Custer was Brevet Major-General of the United States Army, and had fought in nearly a hundred battles, in more than half of which he held important commands. "He never lost a gun or a color, captured more guns, flags, and prisoners than any other general not an army commander."

After the close of the war, General Custer went to the plains with the Seventh Cavalry. Indian warfare was new to him, and his old experience availed him little. His every instinct was for attack, and among the savages they were forced mainly to act on the defensive. His career on the plains was marked by the same qualities which gave him prominence in the Civil War. His greatest exploit was the destruction of Black Kettle's band on the Washita River. His life on the frontier was a succession of narrow escapes. Some of his adventures he has recorded in his "Life on the Plains."

On the 25th of June, 1876, General Custer met his death at the head of his troops. Attacking a large number of Indians at the Little Horn, every member of the five companies of the Seventh Cavalry perished. That he died fighting bravely is proved by the fact that of the dead bodies found on the field of battle, that of the young leader was the only unmutilated one. This is only recorded of one other person, a boy bugler, who had behaved with superhuman bravery in a certain fight, and whose body was left untouched by the savages as a token of respect. General Custer was tall, slender, lithe, and active. While in the Civil War, his love of the romantic and odd led him to adopt an equally conspicuous and picturesque costume—a jaunty jacket and loose breeches of black velvet slashed with gold. High boots, and a broad, shadowy hat completed the striking outfit. On the plains this was replaced by an even more elaborate hunting dress. His hair, which was of a bright golden hue, he wore in long flowing curls.

Very truly yours
R. S. Storrs

RICHARD SALTER STORRS.

The choice New England stock from which the Reverend Dr. Storrs springs "was clerical in its root and branches, sap and leaves." His father was the Reverend Richard Salter Storrs, D.D., of Braintree, Massachusetts. His grandfather, of the same name, was pastor of the Congregational Church of Longmeadow, Connecticut, for nearly forty years. His great-grandfather was the Reverend John Storrs, who was for some time minister of the Congregational Church at East Hampton, Long Island.

The Reverend Dr. Richard S. Storrs was born in Braintree, August 21, 1821. He was graduated at Amherst College in 1839, and was the youngest member of his class. After his graduation, he read law for some months in the office of the celebrated Rufus Choate of Massachusetts, but subsequently entered the Theological Seminary at Andover, from which he was graduated in 1845. He soon after accepted a call to the Harvard Congregational Church at Brookline, Massachusetts. In November of the following year, 1846, he was installed pastor of the Church of the Pilgrims, Brooklyn, New York.

The City of Brooklyn was originally largely settled by New Englanders reared where the Congregational system of church government was more prevalent than any other. In their new home they lost none of their love for their old form of worship. In 1844 the Church of the Pilgrims commenced its existence as an organized body. In July of that year the corner-stone of the imposing stone-church edifice on Brooklyn Heights was laid. It was not dedicated until May 12, 1846. This building, at the time of its erection, surpassed every other structure of the kind in Brooklyn. Imbedded in the façade of the church may be seen a piece of the veritable Plymouth Rock. The edifice is unique in architectural design, and the interior presents a rare illustration of artistic taste and beauty.

When Dr. Storrs was called to the pastorate of the Church of the Pilgrims, he was in the twenty-sixth year of his age. From the time of his entrance upon his duties, there was a steady increase in the attendance, and he now has charge of a large, wealthy, and intelligent congregation. For many years he has evinced great interest in the educational movements of Brooklyn. He took an active part in the establishment of the Packer Institute and in the school established by the late Reverend Dr. Alonzo Gray on the Heights. He is not without literary reputation. When the "Independent" newspaper was commenced in 1848, he became one of the associate editors, and retained the position till 1861. He has also published a number of sermons, orations, addresses; and an elaborate review of the revision of the English version of the Bible, under the auspices of the American Bible Society; also "Graham Lectures on the Power, Wisdom, and Goodness of God, as manifested in the Constitution of the Human Soul;" "Life and Letters of Reverend Daniel Temple;" lectures on "The Conditions of Success in Preaching without Notes;" and has been a frequent contributor to various leading American periodicals.

"Dr. Storrs writes with evident care, and in the well-selected terms of a highly cultivated literary taste. He has been very successful as an editor, and discusses occurring religious and secular topics with readiness and skill. In his sermons he is scholarly and eloquent. As compositions they are replete with merit, and many of them should be classed as magnificent orations. The historical and other facts are introduced in a most pleasing and interesting form, and, where he indulges in fancy, it is not only truly poetic, but both original and sensible. As a preacher he has some striking peculiarities. His appearance is dignified and solemn, and his delivery is slow, emphatic, and impressive. His voice is strong, but beautifully modulated and highly sensitive to the emotions. Decided and emphatic in all utterances of fact and opinion, showing a most thorough scholarship in both theology and literature, his sermons are also most touching expressions of Christian sentiment. If the hearer desires to listen to the most polished diction, to original and great thoughts of a scholarly as well as practical mind, he will be fully gratified; but in no case, should he be seeking the way of eternal life, will he fail to be told the right path. Thus, while scholarship and oratory are attractive features of the ministrations of Dr. Storrs, both are made subservient to his greater aim, the regeneration of his fellow-men."

Dr. Storrs has a large, tall, and stately form. His face is characteristic of intelligence and goodness. "A representative of the most advanced culture of the American pulpit, he is equally an example of the stern and higher virtues, which are at once the strength and safety of society."

CALEB CUSHING.

CALEB CUSHING descends from an old colonial family, of political, judicial, and military distinction, and was born in Salisbury, Massachusetts, January 17, 1800. He was graduated at Harvard College in 1817, and was subsequently a tutor of mathematics and natural philosophy in that university. He then studied law at Cambridge, was admitted to the bar in 1822, and commenced practice at Newburyport; and he also became a prominent contributor to the "North American Review," writing chiefly upon historical and legal subjects. In 1825-6 he served in the State Legislature, and in 1829 visited Europe, publishing, on his return, "Reminiscences of Spain," and an able "Historical and Political Review of the Revolution in France."

Mr. Cushing was again elected to the Massachusetts Legislature in 1833, retaining that position until 1835, when he represented the Essex district in Congress, where he served four consecutive terms. During the administration of President Tyler he was one of the few Whigs who sustained the course of the President in abandoning his political friends; and since that time he has been connected with the Democratic party. In 1843 he was sent, by the President, Commissioner to China, and empowered to negotiate the first treaty between that Empire and the United States. In 1844 the conditions of the treaty were concluded with the Emperor of China, and, in view of the commercial advantages thus secured to the United States, Mr. Cushing's mission was esteemed a great success. On his return home in 1846, he was again elected to the Massachusetts Legislature, and, during the session of 1847, was a prominent advocate of the Mexican war. Failing to induce the Legislature to aid in equipping a volunteer regiment, he furnished the requisite means; was chosen Colonel of the regiment, joined General Taylor on the Rio Grande, in the spring of 1847, and soon after received the appointment of Brigadier-General. While still in Mexico, he was nominated for Governor of Massachusetts by the Democrats, but was defeated. In 1850, for the sixth time, Mr. Cushing represented Newburyport in the Legislature of Massachusetts. In the same year he was elected the first Mayor of that city, and was re-elected the following year. In 1851 he was made Justice of the Supreme Court of Massachusetts, which position he filled until 1853, when President Pierce appointed him United States Attorney-General, from which office he retired March 4, 1857. In 1857-8-9 he again served in the Legislature of Massachusetts.

The National Democratic Convention assembled at Charleston, S. C., in April, 1860, for the purpose of nominating their Presidential ticket. The presiding officer on that occasion was Caleb Cushing. The circumstances were grave; the conflicting opinions and interests of the Northern and Southern Democracy — Douglas and anti-Douglas — there represented were beyond reconciliation. The Convention broke up, and with it the party. In the following June the seceders from that body met at Baltimore, and nominated John C. Breckinridge for President. From this division in the Democratic party circumstances resulted that eventually culminated in the election of Abraham Lincoln as President. Then followed the long and terrible civil war.

Throughout the struggle Mr. Cushing kept aloof from party action, but supported the war measures of the Government in the Legislature of Massachusetts, to which he was again elected for two successive terms. Subsequently he was appointed by President Lincoln to represent the Government before the united Commission formed to determine certain claims of Great Britain against the United States. In 1866 President Johnson appointed him one of the three Commissioners to revise and codify the laws of the United States. These occupations were interrupted in 1867-8 by the special mission which he assumed from this Government to the United States of Colombia.

In 1872, during President Grant's administration, Mr. Cushing was appointed one of the Counsel of the United States on the Alabama claims, before the High Tribunal of Arbitration, convened at Geneva, Switzerland. On his return from Europe he published a history of the arbitration, entitled "The Treaty of Washington; its Negotiation, Execution, and Discussion relating thereto," which elicited grave comment both at home and abroad, by its criticism of the character and conduct of Sir Alexander Cockburn, the British Arbitrator. In December, 1873, he received the appointment of Minister to Spain.

Mr. Cushing died at Newburyport, Mass., January 2, 1879, in fulness of years, for he was as old as the century. His literary, historical, and political productions, as well as his orations and addresses, have been very numerous. He was an attractive and able speaker, a remarkable conversationalist, a thorough scholar, and a fine linguist.

ROSCOE CONKLING.

The Hon. Roscoe Conkling, United States Senator, was born in Albany, N. Y., on the 30th of October, 1829. His father, the Hon. Alfred Conkling, LL.D., an eminent jurist and legal author, was graduated at Union College, admitted to the bar in 1812, and soon ranked among the prominent lawyers of his native State. He was for several years District Attorney of Montgomery Co., N. Y., and was also a Representative of that district in the Seventeenth Congress. Subsequent to the termination of his congressional term, Mr. Conkling was appointed, by President John Q. Adams, United States Judge for the Northern District of New York, a position he retained for nearly a quarter of a century. Upon resigning this office, Judge Conkling was appointed by President Fillmore United States Minister to the Mexican Republic. The mother of Senator Conkling was Eliza Cockburn, who was born at Rhinebeck, Dutchess Co., N. Y. She was the daughter of James Cockburn, a native of Scotland, and a scientifically educated civil engineer. Her maternal grandfather, Col. Hendrick Frey, was of German descent, a man of high social position and the owner of a large landed estate in the valley of the Mohawk. Col. Frey married Gertrude Herkimer, a sister of General Herkimer, of revolutionary fame. Mrs. Conkling's literary taste and culture were indicated by the name she gave her son, who was called for the celebrated English author, Wm. Roscoe, as well as in that selected by her for Judge Conkling's beautiful suburban residence in the vicinity of Auburn, N. Y., which bore the name of "Melrose," in honor of the famous abbey of the country of her ancestors.

Roscoe Conkling received a good academic education, and at an early age entered the law office of J. A. Spencer, of Utica. In 1850, after being admitted to the bar, Mr. Conkling was appointed, by the Governor of the State, District Attorney of Oneida County, N. Y. Despite his youth, the duties of the office were never more skilfully and energetically discharged. The citizens of Utica recognized his unusual abilities by electing him Mayor of that city in 1858, and the public records proved him to be the youngest person who had held that office. At the close of his municipal term, he was elected to the House of Representatives for the Thirty-sixth Congress, and was also re-elected to the Thirty-seventh Congress, of which his brother, the Hon. Frederick A. Conkling, a prominent merchant of New York City, was also a member. During each of these congressional sessions, he served as Chairman of the Committee on the District of Columbia, and also as Chairman of a Special Committee on the Bankrupt Law.

Mr. Conkling was also elected a Representative to the Thirty-ninth Congress, serving with distinction on the Committee of Ways and Means, and on the Joint Committee on Reconstruction. He was re-elected for the following term, but, before the opening of the Fortieth Congress, the Legislature of the State of New York elected him to the Senate of the United States, as the successor of the Hon. Ira Harris. He entered upon his six years' official term in March, 1867, and at its expiration was re-elected, taking his seat in 1873. During the Fortieth Congress he served in the Senate as Chairman of the Committee on the Revision of the Laws of the United States, and was a member of the Committee on Judiciary and Commerce. His efforts were especially prominent in the work of Reconstruction, and he advocated the resolution submitting the Suffrage Amendment. In the famous impeachment trial of Andrew Johnson, he voted with the majority in favor of conviction. The bill providing for the erection of the Post-Office building in New York City was presented by Senator Conkling.

In the National Republican Convention held at Cincinnati in 1876, Senator Conkling's name was prominently mentioned in connection with the nomination for the Presidency; and he had many supporters both in and out of the Convention.

He was appointed one of the select committee of the Senate "to take into consideration the state of the law respecting the ascertaining and declaration of the result of the election of President and Vice-President." His speech on the 23d and 24th of January, 1877, in relation to the bill "to provide for and regulate the counting of the votes," in the recent Presidential campaign, was one of the most impressive delivered on that subject.

Senator Conkling is somewhat over six feet in stature, broad-shouldered, deep-chested, and well-formed. His general physical characteristics betoken his Scotch lineage. He has many years been distinguished by eloquence and power as an orator, by profound legal skill and knowledge, and as a prominent leader in the national councils.

HENRY WAGER HALLECK.

Major-General Henry Wager Halleck, of the United States Army, was a son of the Honorable Joseph H. Halleck, and grandson of Peter Halleck, of Long Island Revolutionary memory. He was born at Waterville, Oneida County, N. Y., January 15, 1815. After pursuing the usual course of study, he entered the Military Academy at West Point in 1835. He was graduated in 1839, ranking third in his class, and was breveted Second-Lieutenant of Engineers July 1. From that time to June, 1840, he served in the Academy as Assistant Professor of Engineering. From that time until 1845 he was engaged as Assistant Engineer upon the fortifications in the harbor of New York. He was then sent by the General Government to examine the principal military establishments in Europe. He also, during the same year, delivered a course of lectures in Boston on "Military Science and Art," which he collected in one volume in 1846, prefixing an essay on the "Justifiableness of War." "No pretension," says the author in his preface, "is made to originality in any part of the work; the sole object having been to embody, in a small compass, well-established military principles, and to illustrate these by reference to the events of past history, and the opinions and practice of the best generals."

During the war with Mexico, Lieutenant Halleck served in Lower California and on the Pacific, and was breveted Captain for gallant conduct. During the military governments of Kearny, Mason, and Riley, from 1847 to the close of 1849, he was Secretary of State for the Territory of California. He was chief of Commodore Shubrick's staff during 1847 and 1848, and in 1849 was a member of the convention to form, and of the committee to draft, the constitution of the State of California. He was also Judge-Advocate and Inspector of Lighthouses, and General Director of the New Almaden Quicksilver Mines. In July, 1853, he was promoted to a full Captaincy of Engineers; but he was already indentified with the interests of the Golden State, and finally resigned his position in the army August 1, 1854.

HENRY WAGER HALLECK.

Perfecting his legal studies, he soon became a leading member of the San Francisco bar, and the firm of "Halleck, Billings & Co." became synonymous with victory in the legal battles of the California courts. The breaking out of the civil war found him enjoying a lucrative practice. He, however, closed his business and offered his services to the War Department. On the recommendation of Lieutenant-General Scott, the President appointed him a Major-General of the Regular Army of the United States.

In November, 1861, General Fremont was removed from the command of the Department of the West, and Halleck was appointed his successor. His headquarters were established at St. Louis, from which, as a base of operations, he directed the military movements in the State. Early in April, 1862, he took command of the army before Corinth, the investment of which was soon followed by its capture. Shortly after this event General Halleck was summoned to Washington as General-in-Chief of the Armies of the United States. Relinquishing his command to Grant and Buell, he hastened to the National Capital. He held the position of General-in-Chief till March 12, 1864. Grant being then made Lieutenant-General, Halleck received the appointment of Chief of Staff in the army, which he held till April, 1865, when he was placed in command of the military division of the James, his headquarters being at Richmond. In the following August he was transferred to the division of the Pacific, and in March, 1869, to that of the South, his headquarters being at Louisville.

General Halleck published several works upon military and scientific topics, the principal of which are: "Bitumen, its Varieties, Properties, and Uses;" "Elements of Military Art and Science," a second edition of which was published some years after, with critical notes on the Mexican and Crimean wars; "The Mining Laws of Spain and Mexico;" a translation, with an introduction, of "De Fooz on the Law of Mines;" "International Laws, or the Rules regulating the Intercourse of States in Peace and War;" a translation, with notes, of Jomini's "Life of Napoleon;" and "A Treatise on International Law and the Laws of War, prepared for the Use of Schools and Colleges."

General Halleck died in Louisville, Kentucky, January 9, 1872. He attained a high reputation for intellectual ability, and was officially distinguished for sagacity, energy, patriotism, and integrity. Though rather below the medium height, his personal appearance and martial bearing favorably impressed the observer.

RUFUS CHOATE.

Rufus Choate, LL.D., was born October 1, 1799, in the old town of Ipswich, Massachusetts. He was a descendant of a race of thrifty farmers settled for more than a century in that thriftiest of regions— New England. His father was a man of no ordinary ability, and his mother was in every respect an estimable lady. The father died before the boy was nine years of age, and the entire care of directing his education fell upon Mrs. Choate. He began the study of Latin at the age of ten; and continued in that and other studies during a portion of each year with the parish clergyman or teachers of the district schools. In the summer of 1815, he entered the Freshman class in Dartmouth College. After his graduation with the highest honors of his class, he was retained as tutor in the college for one year.

Upon the close of his short experience as an instructor, Mr. Choate began the preliminary studies of his chosen profession, that of the law. Entering the Dane Law School at Cambridge, he spent a few months there and then entered the law office of the well-known author, lawyer, and orator, William Wirt, at Washington. After a profitable year spent under the direction of Mr. Wirt, young Mr. Choate returned from the South and completed his legal studies with Judge Cummins of Salem. He was admitted to the bar and commenced the practice of his profession in Danvers in 1824. After two or three years he removed to Salem, where, by the exercise of his remarkable talents, he soon became favorably known as a rising lawyer. He already manifested the legal acuteness, judgment, and tact, for which he afterwards became so celebrated. In 1825 Mr. Choate was called to fill his first public office, that of Representative to the Massachusetts Legislature, and in 1827 he was in the Senate of the same State. The sagacious and energetic part he took in the debates during these terms of service, won him a widespread reputation. In 1832 he was elected a Member of Congress from the Essex District, and was re-elected in 1834. He served one session, and then resigning, went to Boston where he devoted himself to his profession. From this time he rose steadily to the high position as lawyer and orator, which rightly belongs to him among noteworthy Americans. The leading men of the bar regarded with respect and admiration the great mind they saw beneath some peculiarities of manner. "Mr. Choate," says his biographer, Professor Brown, " whose appearance and manner were unique, whose eloquence then was as exuberant, fervid, and rich as it ever became; who, however modest for himself, was bold almost to rashness for his client; who startled court and jury by his vehemence, and confounded the common-place and routine lawyer by the novelty and brilliancy of his tactics; who, free from vulgar tricks, was yet full of surprises, and though perpetually delighting by the novelty and beauty of his argument, was yet without conceit or vanity, could not at once be fully understood and appreciated. He fairly fought his way to eminence, created the taste which he gratified, and demonstrated the possibility of almost a new variety of eloquence."

In 1841, on the retirement of Daniel Webster from the United States Senate, Mr. Choate was chosen to fill the vacancy. During his Senatorship he spoke ably and forcibly on the McLeod case, the Fiscal Bank Bill, Oregon, the Smithsonian Institute (of which he was a regent), and in opposition to the annexation of Texas. At the close of his term he gave himself up wholly to his profession. After the death of the illustrious Mr. Webster, he was the acknowledged leader of the Massachusetts bar. In 1855 Mr. Choate met with an accident which seriously impaired his health. After suffering during portions of four years, he sailed for Europe with the hope of recruiting his strength. On the way he became so ill that he was obliged to stop at Halifax, Nova Scotia, where he died, July 13, 1859.

Mr. Choate was tall and commanding in person, with a remarkably expressive face, and a rich and musical voice. His powers of reasoning and imagination were great, and he excelled in wit and fancy. He was a profound student of literature, art, and science. His legal reputation was firmly established. "In the management of causes he possessed consummate tact and unerring judgment. Skillful in the examination of witnesses, never making a mistake himself nor overlooking one in an opponent, his powers as a lawyer were seen to the greatest advantage in the unpremeditated discussion of the law-points that incidentally arose."

FERNANDO DE SOTO.

"Of all the enterprises undertaken in the spirit of wild adventure none has surpassed, for hardihood and variety of incident, that of the renowned Fernando De Soto and his band of cavaliers. As Mr. Irving observes: 'It was poetry put into action; it was the knight-errantry of the Old World carried into the depths of the American wilderness. The personal adventures, the feats of individual prowess, the picturesque descriptions of steel-clad cavaliers with lance and helm, and prancing steed, glittering through the wildernesses of Florida, Georgia, Alabama, and the prairies of the "Far West," would seem to us mere fictions of romance did they not come to us in the matter-of-fact narratives of those who were eye-witnesses, and who recorded minute memoranda of every day's incidents.'"

Fernando De Soto was born at Xeres de los Caballeros, in Estremadura, about 1500. "Of a noble but reduced family he was enabled, by the favor of Pedrarias Davila, to spend several years at one of the universities, and distinguished himself in literary studies, and especially in athletic accomplishments. In 1519 he accompanied his patron on his second expedition to America as governor of Darien, and was the most intrepid opponent of the oppressive administration of that officer. He supported Hernandez, in Nicaragua, in 1527, who perished by the hand of Davila in consequence of not heeding his advice. Withdrawing from the service of Davila, he explored, in 1528, the coast of Guatemala and Yucatan for seven hundred miles in search of the strait which was supposed to connect the two oceans. In 1532 De Soto joined Pizarro in his enterprise for conquering Peru. Being sent in 1533 with fifty horsemen and a few targeteers, to explore the highlands of Peru, he penetrated through a pass in the mountains and discovered the great road which led to the Peruvian capital, and was soon after selected by Pizarro to visit the Inca Atahualpa as ambassador. After the capture of the Inca, and when the latter had paid an immense sum for ransom, De Soto in vain expostulated with Pizarro for treacherously refusing to release the Peruvian monarch. He was prominent in the engagements which completed the conquest of Peru, and was the hero of the battle which resulted in the capture of Cuzco, the metropolis. He soon after returned to Spain, met a flattering reception from the emperor Charles V., and married the daughter of Davila, to whom he had long been attached."

In 1536 America was to the Spaniards a land of magnificent promise. Men of the highest rank and culture left their homes and positions and flocked to the new world. Up to this date, however, most of the expeditions had resulted disastrously. De Soto, undismayed by these failures, proposed to the emperor to undertake the conquest of Florida at his own expense, and early in April, 1536, with a large company of choice men, set sail from Spain. They were provided with everything that could possibly be necessary for conquest or for planting colonies. After stopping at Santiago de Cuba and Havana, where the ladies attached to the expedition were left, they crossed the Gulf of Mexico and anchored in the bay of Espiritu Santo, in May, 1539. Two months later De Soto sent all their ships back to Havana. The first year they marched and wandered through East Florida and in Georgia. The Indians they encountered on their route had been rendered hostile by the treatment they had met at the hands of the unfortunate Spanish invader Narvaez. One of his followers, who had been in slavery since the time of his leader's expedition, was captured by De Soto, and from that time served as his interpreter. Month after month the credulous and ambitious procession strolled through the wilderness in the vain hope of finding gold. The Indians constantly deluded them by stories of gold regions several miles further on, and several severe battles were fought. These engagements and the hardships they endured perceptibly diminished their numbers. At last, in the third year of their wanderings (1541), they emerged upon the banks of the Mississippi. They crossed it, and after marching to the mountainous region north of the Arkansas, returned to the "Great Father of Waters." Here, De Soto, who had been the life of the company, sickened and died, in 1542. The exact date of his death is uncertain. To conceal their loss from their enemies, the natives, his followers sank his body, wrapped in his mantle, in the river at midnight.

"He had crossed a large part of the continent and found nothing so remarkable as his burial place."

When he died the remnant of his army were only anxious to reach home in safety. Constructing rude boats they descended the river, and after various adventures reached the settlements in Mexico.

JOHN BLOOMFIELD JERVIS.

TIMOTHY JERVIS was one of the early settlers of Rome, Oneida County, New York. Here for a time he carried on his trade, that of a carpenter, and then turned his attention to farming. His son, John B. Jervis, afterward a distinguished civil engineer, was born December 14, 1795, at Huntington, Long Island. His boyhood was spent in Rome with his father, assisting in the daily labor of the farm. He attended a district school until he was fifteen years of age, when he left his books to commence life as a farmer, which it then seemed he was destined to make his permanent occupation. When about twenty-two years of age a circumstance occurred which, though apparently trifling, eventually decided his future career. Ground had been broken for the great Erie Canal in July, 1817. The general survey of the engineers having laid the route through the village of Rome, it became necessary to locate the line through a piece of cedar swamp in the vicinity. Young Jervis and one of his father's axemen were called upon to assist in the work for a few days. His own words will best narrate how this incident led to his becoming a civil engineer: "Myself and assistant were expert axemen, and, with the enthusiasm of a new and untried operation, we entered upon the work. In the course of proceeding it often happened that I was brought to wait a little time with the rod-man (as he was called), or target-bearer. At such times I was led to examine the target and notice the operations. I began to think I could do that duty, and so thoughts rambled in my mind of learning the art. At the last day of this service, I ventured, half jest and half earnest, to ask the principal,—What will you give me to go with you next year and carry one of those rods? To this he replied that he would give me twelve dollars per month. With some trepidation this engagement was settled, and I occupied such evenings and other times as my daily avocations permitted, in the study of surveying—the art at that time regarded as the basis of civil engineering."

After a few months' experience, Mr. Jervis was, in the spring of

1819, appointed resident engineer of a party engaged upon a portion of the middle division in Madison and Onondaga counties. From that time to the completion and formal opening of the Erie Canal in 1825, he was attached to the working force in various official positions. In March of that year he accepted the position of Principal Assistant Engineer of the Delaware and Hudson Canal and Railway Company, which projected a line of communication to connect the coal mines of the Lackawanna Valley with New York City. A personal examination of the country resulted in his favoring an independent canal throughout. This was completed in 1828. In 1830 Mr. Jervis, who had become Chief Engineer of the company, resigned the position, to superintend the construction of a railroad from Albany to Schenectady, which is now an important section of the New York Central route.

In 1836 Mr. Jervis received an invitation from the commissioners of the projected great aqueduct of New York City, to become the Chief Engineer of the enterprise. He accepted the charge, and for six years was actively engaged in his engineering duties. The Croton Dam, the Sing Sing and High Bridges, the distributing reservoir in Forty-second Street, New York City, and the prominent features of the Croton Aqueduct, are his productions. He next directed the Cochituate Water Works at Boston, which were finished under his advice as Consulting Engineer in 1848. About the same time he was appointed Chief Engineer of the projected line to Albany of the Hudson River Railroad Company. In August, 1849, he resigned the position, but was retained as Consulting Engineer.

In 1850 Mr. Jervis spent four months in Europe, most of the time in England. During his visit he was so fortunate as to be present at the launch of one of the large tubes of the magnificent bridge over the Menai Straits. Upon his return to the United States he directed the construction of the remaining link of the Michigan Southern and Northern Illinois Railroad. In 1851, as President of the Chicago and Rock Island Railroad, he commenced that important line. In 1861 he was appointed general superintendent of the Pittsburg, Fort Wayne & Chicago Railroad. He retained this position for more than two years, and continued to act as engineer till 1866. Since that date he has not engaged in the active pursuit of his profession.

The honorary degree of LL.D. was conferred upon him by Hamilton College on the 27th of June, 1878.

Mr. Jervis is the author of a treatise on "Railway Property," and a little volume entitled "The Question of Labor and Capital."

SILAS HORTON STRINGHAM.

REAR-ADMIRAL SILAS H. STRINGHAM, of the United States Navy, was born in Middletown, Orange County, New York, November 7, 1798. After receiving a fair education, he entered the navy as a midshipman in 1809, and was ordered to the "President," under Commodore Rogers, and for the succeeding four years found naval life no holiday sport. He was on board the "President" during the memorable fight on the 16th of May, 1811, with the English corvette "Little Belt," which was one of the immediate causes of the war of 1812.

In 1814 he became lieutenant, and was ordered to the "Spark," of Commodore Decatur's Algerine squadron. In 1817 he was transferred to the "Erie," and in the fall of 1818 to the "Peacock." In 1819 he was ordered to the "Cyane," and convoyed the ship "Elizabeth," which carried to the African coast the first settlers to the future Republic of Liberia. On their arrival, each lieutenant was put in command of a boat to board vessels supposed to be slavers. Capturing four of them, he was made prize-commodore, and sent home in charge of the prizes. In 1821 he was ordered to the sloop-of-war "Hornet" as first lieutenant, and on the West India station captured a notorious pirate ship and slaver. In 1822 he was ordered to the "Cyane," which formed a part of the Mediterranean squadron. He was employed at the Brooklyn Navy Yard from 1825 to 1829; then assigned to the "Peacock," and sent in search of the missing "Hornet," and while engaged in the search was transferred to the sloop "Falmouth" as commander, and sent to Carthagena. Returning to New York in 1830, the next five years were spent in shore service; and in 1835 he was ordered to the command of the "John Adams." In 1837 he was appointed second in command at the Brooklyn Navy Yard. In 1842 he received his commission as captain in the navy, to date from September 8, 1841. He was then ordered to the "Independence." In 1843 he was appointed commander of the Brooklyn Navy Yard, where he remained till 1846.

SILAS HORTON STRINGHAM.

At the commencement of the Mexican War, Captain Stringham was ordered to the "Ohio," and sailed from Boston to Vera Cruz. He took an active part in the bombardment of the fortress of San Juan de Ulloa. After the reduction of the fort, the "Ohio" returned to New York, and on her way called at Havana, being the first American ship-of-the-line which had ever entered that port. In 1851 he was made commander of the Norfolk Navy Yard, and in April, 1852, was assigned to the command of the Mediterranean squadron. In 1855 he returned to the United States, and was assigned to the command of the Charlestown Navy Yard, which he held until May, 1859, when he was allowed a little respite from active duty.

In March, 1861, he was ordered to Washington as member of a naval court-martial, and on special duty, and while there was appointed flag-officer of the Atlantic blockading squadron, and ordered to the "Minnesota" as his flag-ship. He was honored with the preparation of the first of those combined naval and military expeditions which have crowned the American navy with such glory. On the 26th of August, the fleet sailed from Hampton Roads for Hatteras Inlet. On the morning of the 28th an attack was made upon the forts, and the bombardment of Fort Clark was continued until half-past one P.M., when both forts hauled down their flags, and the garrison of Fort Clark escaped to Fort Hatteras. The fleet ceased firing, and the "Monticello" was sent into the inlet to discover whether the forts intended to surrender. When within six hundred yards of Fort Hatteras, the occupants of that fort commenced firing upon her. Perceiving this, Stringham went to her assistance with the "Wabash," "Susquehanna," and "Minnesota," and soon compelled them to cease firing. The next morning the fleet renewed its firing upon Fort Hatteras. About eleven o'clock a white flag was displayed from the fort, and the preliminaries having been agreed upon, the garrison, consisting of seven hundred and fifteen men, surrendered to Flag-Officer Stringham and General Butler who commanded the land forces. For this affair Flag-Officer Stringham received the thanks of the Government. In September, 1861, he was, at his own request, relieved from his command. In July, 1862, he was made a rear-admiral on the retired list. During the year 1863 he was assigned to the Charlestown Navy Yard as commandant of the station, and was thus employed during the remainder of the war.

Rear-Admiral Stringham died at his home in Brooklyn, New York, February 7, 1876. At the time of his death he was Port Admiral of the port of New York, which position he had held since 1867.

THOMAS ALEXANDER SCOTT.

Thomas Alexander Scott is one of the most prominent men who have been engaged in the service and management of public railways. He was born in Loudon, Franklin County, Pennsylvania, on the 28th of December, 1823, and received his education at the village district school of that place. When ten years old he left his books, and began work in a country store, and was employed in three different towns until 1841. He then entered a collector's office at Columbia, Pennsylvania, as a clerk under the Board of Canal Commissioners, and continued in that capacity there, and in Philadelphia, for several years.

In 1851 he became connected with the Pennsylvania Railroad Company, one of the leading railway corporations of the United States. He was on duty first at Hollidaysburg, then an important shipping-point between the railroad and the canal, and was afterwards placed in charge of the business of the Company passing over the Portage Road and the Western Division of the State Canal. Upon the completion of the Western Division of the railroad he was appointed its Superintendent. He continued in that position until 1858, when he was made General Superintendent of the line from Philadelphia to Pittsburg. In 1860, on the death of Mr. William B. Foster, Vice-President of the Company, he was elected to succeed him.

During the ensuing ten years the Pennsylvania Railroad increased greatly in length; new branches and leased roads came under its control, and the traffic grew rapidly. "The prosperity of this great corporation has been shared with the State whose name it bears. Local interests have been fostered, local business encouraged, and everything possible done to show that the interests of the people and the railway were inseparable, and that the advantage of the one was the profit of the other. Branches have been built into the valleys to develop the iron, coal, lumber, oil, and other resources of the State, which have added largely to its wealth, and also served to feed the main line; and the same wise foresight has been quick to perceive the value of connecting lines, and, by timely securing them, control the trade of large sections of country, and bring increased earnings to the parent company. By purchase or lease, many leading interests within the State of Pennsylvania have been harmonized, and the Northern Central, Cumberland Valley, Philadelphia and Erie, the Erie and Pittsburgh, and other lines are thus worked with the utmost economy and efficiency to secure one general result. Outside the State this same policy has necessitated at times the most prompt and decisive action; and in these emergencies the singularly clear perception and executive ability of Mr. Scott have shown to rare advantage."

In the fall of 1861 Mr. Scott became Assistant-Secretary of War, and as such directed the transportation of our armies. He directed the reconstruction of the road from Annapolis, which opened communication with, and did much to aid the troops that saved the National Capital. He served in this capacity under Secretaries Cameron and Stanton till the fall of 1862, when he returned to Philadelphia. He was again called into service by Secretary Stanton, after the battle of Chickamauga, to go to Louisville and aid in the movement of the Eleventh and Twelfth Corps by the way of Nashville, to the relief of Rosecrans at Chattanooga. The Army of the Tennessee was so reinforced as to be able to drive in full retreat the enemy who had held it in so perilous a position.

About 1870 Mr. Scott became President of the Union Pacific Railroad and of the Texas Pacific Railroad Company.

On the 3d of June, 1874, Mr. Scott was elected President of the Pennsylvania Railroad Company, to succeed Mr. Thomson, who died in May of that year.

With all the labor, however, thus thrown upon him, he has the happy faculty of rapid business dispatch; and when the work is once done he is able to dismiss it utterly, and on leaving his office to leave all business cares behind him. This is partly due to a vigorous physique, which seems to defy toil, and also to an elastic temperament, which never regrets what is unalterable, but is ever busy in devising new schemes to accomplish a desired end.

EPES SARGENT.

Epes Sargent, author and journalist, was born in Gloucester, Massachusetts, September 27, 1812. In early childhood his family removed to Boston, where he entered the public Latin school. He pursued his studies there for five years, with the exception of six months which were spent in a visit to Europe with his father. After his return home he and half a dozen other boys started a small weekly paper called the Literary Journal. In it he published some account of his experience in Russia. He entered Harvard University, but did not graduate.

Mr. Sargent became editorially engaged at an early age. Commencing with his first boyish efforts in the Literary Journal and the Collegian, a Harvard monthly, he has since been connected with The Token, Parley's Magazine, The New England Magazine, The Boston Daily Advertiser, the Boston Atlas, the New York Mirror, the New Monthly Magazine, the Boston Transcript, and the School Monthly. He has also contributed to the Knickerbocker, the Atlantic Monthly, and other periodicals. He assisted Mr. S. G. Goodrich in the preparation of his Geography, and several of the " Peter Parley " books.

Mr. Sargent edited the Poetical Works of Thomas Campbell, with Memoirs and Notes. He also edited the works and memoirs of the following poets: Collins, Gray, and Goldsmith, all in one volume; Samuel Rogers, Thomas Hood, and Horace and James Smith. The Modern Acting Drama was published under his supervision for ten years. Also Selections in Poetry, Select Works of Benjamin Franklin, including his Autobiography, with Memoir and Notes. The Memoir, including the Autobiography, was afterward published separately.

Mr. Sargent is widely known as an author. Among his works are: " Wealth and Worth; or, Which Make the Man?" " What's to be Done? or The Will and The Way;" " The Life and Services of Henry Clay," said to have been preferred by Mr. Clay to any other life of him; "The Mariner's Library;" "American Adventure by Land and Sea;" "The Critic Criticised; a Reply to a Review of Webster's Orthographical System in the Democratic Review;" "Arctic Adventure by Sea and Land;" "Original Dialogues;" "Fleetwood;" "Planchette; or, the Despair of Science: an Account of Modern Spiritualism;" and "Peculiar: A Tale of the Great Transition." He has published anonymously a number of prose works.

Mr. Sargent is the author of a series of five Readers for schools, followed by Primer, Intermediate books, and Spelling-books, and of the Standard Speaker, the Intermediate Standard Speaker, and the Primary Standard Speaker. The success which they met with was due to the great care bestowed upon them, and the good taste with which they were executed.

Mr. Sargent has written several very successful plays. In 1836 he wrote for Miss Josephine Clifton a five-act play, entitled "The Bride of Genoa." The next year he wrote for Miss Ellen Tree the tragedy of "Velasco." His other plays are "Change makes Change," a comedy; and "The Priestess," a tragedy in five acts.

As a poet Mr. Sargent will be long remembered, especially as the composer of "A Life on the Ocean Wave," which for many years has been a favorite with all classes. In 1849 an edition of his poems was published, under the title, "Songs of the Sea and other Poems." It is composed chiefly of a number of spirited lyrics, several of which have been set to music. A series of sonnets is included, "Shells and Seaweeds: Records of a Summer Voyage to Cuba." "It evinces a fine fancy, with keen appreciation of the beautiful in natural scenery." In 1869 he published "The Woman who Dared: A Poem."

As a lecturer, Mr. Sargent has been widely known before the Mercantile Library Association of Boston, and similar associations in the Middle and Eastern States.

John Osborn Sargent, a brother of Epes Sargent, was a well-known lawyer, journalist, and author.

HORATIO SEYMOUR.

The ancestors of the Honorable Horatio Seymour, one of the most distinguished citizens of the State of New York, were among the earliest settlers in Hartford, Connecticut. During the Revolutionary war, Moses Seymour distinguished himself as an officer in the Connecticut militia. Another member of the family was at one time the Representative of the State of Vermont in the Senate of the United States; while still another represented the State of Connecticut in the same body. Henry Seymour, the father of the Honorable Horatio Seymour, was a native of Connecticut, but removed early in life to Onondaga County, New York, where the son was born May 31, 1811. His wife descended from Colonel Forman, a distinguished soldier of the Revolution.

The early boyhood of the future statesman was spent in his birthplace. When he was seven years of age the family removed to Utica. Soon after the change to the new home, he was sent to a private academy, from which he entered Hobart College, where he remained until his fifteenth year. He next entered the Military Academy at Middletown, Connecticut, from which institution he was graduated with honor. Returning to Utica he entered the office of a well-known attorney of that place. Upon the completion of his legal studies he was admitted to the Oneida bar, and commenced the practice of law in Utica. He was beginning to be very favorably known as a lawyer of fine abilities, when by the death of both his father and father-in-law, he came into possession of a large property. The care of these estates seemed to require his whole time and attention, and he accordingly determined to abandon his profession and devote himself to his private duties.

Many of the most able men of the Seymour family have been strong Democrats. Mr. Horatio Seymour also has always been attached to that party. In 1841 he was chosen to the office of Mayor of Utica, and the same year was elected to the State Assembly by a large majority, and was thrice re-elected. In 1845 he was chosen Speaker of the House. From the time of his entrance upon political life his views upon all questions affecting the people and the affairs of his native State and the nation at large, have been entitled to great weight. In 1846 he retired from office, but continued to take an active interest in politics and to labor for the good of his party, the members of which regarded him with high consideration. In 1850 he received the Democratic nomination for Governor, but was not elected. In 1852 he was again nominated for that office, and was this time successful. In 1854 he received the nomination for the third time, but in the ensuing election was defeated by a small majority.

In the early days of the late Civil War, Mr Seymour assisted in raising troops and forwarding them to the front in defense of the National Government. He was for some time Chairman of the War Committee in Oneida County. In 1862 he was for the fourth time the Democratic candidate for the office of Governor of the State of New York, and was elected. Upon the outbreak of the great riot of July, 1863, in New York City, Governor Seymour hastened to that city, and, repairing at once to the City Hall, addressed the large crowd gathered there to hear him. By his personal popularity he succeeded in finally dispersing the rioters and checking the commotion. He also prevented further trouble by organizing large forces of respectable citizens to assist the police in maintaining public order. He next appealed to the President, urging a suspension of the Draft, that being one of the primary causes of public disturbance. In 1864 Governor Seymour was President of the National Democratic Convention held in Chicago; and in 1868 presided over the one held in New York. In the well-remembered campaign of the last named year his name was brought still more prominently before the people of the United States, having received the Democratic nomination for President. It need not be recorded here that General Grant, the Republican nominee, was elected. In 1875 Horatio Seymour was President of the National Dairymen's Association. Later, he was elected President of the Prison Association of the United States.

Mr. Seymour is a gentleman of dignified personal appearance and genial in manner. In social life he is respected and esteemed for his unimpeachable private character. Even his harshest political opponents concede his high principle and purity of conduct. His long experience in politics has made him a master in the art; while his eloquence and grace as a public speaker, added to his genial disposition, have not only made him a power in his party, but have also secured for him a host of ardent admirers and warm personal friends.

SAMUEL P. HEINTZELMAN.

SAMUEL P. HEINTZELMAN, Major-General of Volunteers, and Brevet Major-General of the Regular Army of the United States, was born September 30, 1805, in Manheim, Lancaster County, Pennsylvania. He is of German descent. His grandfather, who came to this country about the time of Braddock's campaign in the French and Indian war, was the first white settler in Manheim.

S. P. Heintzelman was graduated at the West Point Military Academy in 1826. The same year he was brevetted second lieutenant in the Third Infantry. In 1833 he became first lieutenant in the Second Infantry. He was appointed captain in the Quartermaster's Department United States Army during the Creek war in Alabama. In 1846, when the law passed separating the staff from the line of the army, he resigned his staff commission and went into Mexico as captain of the Second Infantry, and was brevetted major for gallant conduct at the battle of Huamantla. In 1848 he was ordered to California, and assigned the command of the Southern District. In 1850 the Indians became troublesome, but he brought them into subjection, for which service he was brevetted lieutenant-colonel by the President. In 1858 he joined his regiment in Texas as major of the First Infantry. When the Cortinas difficulty broke out, he was ordered to take command of the forces on the Rio Grande. After several engagements with the Mexicans, he dispersed Cortinas' band, and drove them back into Mexico.

Foreseeing the political difficulties of the country, he obtained leave of absence, and reported at Washington in February, 1861. In May he was made Acting Inspector-General of the Department of Washington. He was shortly afterwards made a brigadier-general of volunteers and colonel in the Seventeenth United States Infantry. On May 24, he commanded the first troops that crossed the Potomac into Virginia, and at midnight took possession of Arlington Heights and the surrounding country. He distinguished himself at the battle of Bull Run, where he commanded the extreme right of the army. In this engagement he was severely wounded in the arm. Refusing to leave the field or even to dismount, he only waited to have the bullet cut out and the wound dressed, then putting spurs to his horse, "grim old Heintzelman," as his companions at West Point and in the army delighted to call him, was quickly in the midst of his division, and led it to the last with undiminished courage.

After the reorganization of the Army of the Potomac, and its division into five corps, General Heintzelman was assigned to the command of the third corps, and ordered to the Peninsula. His troops were the first to land there, and were in the advance of the army in its march on Yorktown. In the battle of Williamsburg his divisions gained a complete victory. His commission of major-general of volunteers dated from this battle.

At the battle of Fair Oaks, General Heintzelman with his corps repulsed their foe and drove them back toward their defences at Richmond. For his action in the battle at Seven Pines, which occurred the following day, he was made a brevet brigadier-general in the regular service. Later occurred the Seven Days' battle, in which he fought at Peach Orchard, Savage Station, and Charles City Cross Roads.

After leaving the Peninsula he hastened to the assistance of Pope, and was engaged at the Second Bull Run battle, and at Chantilly. From September, 1862, to February, 1863, he held the command of all the troops and forts south of the Potomac. At the end of that time he was given the Department of Washington, which he retained until October of that year. He was next placed in command of the Northern Department, consisting of the States of Ohio, Indiana, Illinois, and Michigan, with headquarters at Columbus. Early in 1866 he was sent to Texas, and was soon placed in command of the Port of Galveston, and of the Fifth Military District, with headquarters at New Orleans. In 1869 he retired from active service with the full rank of major-general.

"He never shirked a hardship himself, and never inflicted one, except when the exigencies of the service demanded it. Happy in his refined social and domestic relations, his moral influence was always pure, as his charity for the faults of others was broad. Impatient of inaction, hot and impetuous when the battle was on, yet never reckless nor careless of the lives of his men, he had at once the coolness, the determined bravery, the unselfishness, and the *esprit* which go to make the true soldier, and his career must be regarded as one of the most distinguished and successful in the army of the Union."

ELIPHALET NOTT.

ELIPHALET NOTT, D.D., LL.D., was born in the town of Ashford, Windham County, Connecticut, June 25th, 1773.

Despite the straitened circumstances of his parents and the meagre advantages of a backwoods school "keeping" but two months of the winter and distant five miles from his home, his native talent, developed by the care of a mother remarkable alike for intelligence, energy, and piety, early gained for him the respect of the community in which he began his career. At eighteen, while studying Theology, he also filled the Principalship of the Plainfield Academy. His rare knowledge of character, his firm yet genial methods, and his substitution of moral for physical discipline (then quite a new experiment) gained a success which made it doubtful whether education or the ministry would be his greater field of usefulness. The splendid results of his life-work proved him to have had an extraordinary call to both.

In 1796 he proceeded to his field of missionary labor at Cherry Valley in the State of New York. There also he preached and taught school during two years until called to the Presbyterian Church at Albany. He was then but twenty-five years old. The master-minds of the law and of statesmanship, the popular representatives from all portions of the State, such men as Hamilton, Spencer, Kent, Clinton, were regular or frequent attendants on his preaching; as also were the young of all denominations. His fine presence and delivery, his clearness in the development of his theme suggesting, if not suggested by, the admirable French models, his passages of vivid description and ardent appeal produced an impression second probably to no other pulpit oratory in our country in that day.

After six years of ministry in Albany, Mr. Nott was called to the Presidency of Union College. He found the institution possessing a small Faculty, only forty students and no pecuniary resources. By common consent of its Trustees and Faculty, the selection of teachers, the direction of courses of study, the management of finances, the erection of buildings were left with complete confidence to his sagacity, tact and taste. Long before it was thought of elsewhere, he introduced into the curriculum the Scientific course, which has since become a prominent feature in every college. Laboring for Union with unwearying persistence, he justified the words of Dr. Tayler Lewis, calling him "the first of College presidents, the founder and guardian genius of this institution." In ten years its numbers had increased fivefold, and on his retirement from presidential duties its property was valued at half a million.

Amid these various labors Doctor Nott made time to aid every movement for the good of society. On Sundays, he would drive out to some little country congregation near, to preach to them; and he often expressed his happiness in such simple, humble work for the Master. His visits to the large cities always, of course, brought invitations to their most prominent pulpits. In his advocacy of the better observance of the Sabbath, he lectured, wrote, and organized individual effort. He labored earnestly for the rights of the negro; and but for some untoward action of the extreme abolitionists, he would have completed, in connection with several eminent statesmen, a scheme for abolishing slavery without civil convulsion or considerable disturbance to Southern interests. He was among the first to preach and to practise Total Abstinence. The great Common School system of this State owes its establishment to no one person more largely than to President Nott. His counsel on important ecclesiastical and political movements was often sought by their leaders; by Bishop Alonzo Potter (his son-in-law) regarding the administration of his diocese; by Secretary Wm. H. Seward, in the frequent difficulties of his own public career and in grave national crises. The material comfort of community also owes a great debt to those persistent experiments which produced the base-burning stove and several improvements in machinery.

Endowed with a sound physique, always simple in his food, abstaining totally during most of his life from all stimulants (including tobacco), a hard and willing worker, President Nott retained good general health and mental vigor till he was eighty-six years old. His last sermon was preached on Thanksgiving Day of 1860. After some years marked by frequent suffering—a suffering accepted with humble trust and soothed by a wifely devotion which knew no rest through day or night—he departed this life at Union College, January 29th, 1866.

JOHN JAY.

THROUGHOUT the successive generations of two centuries, the name of Jay has been an honored one. Pierre Jay, a Huguenot merchant of New Rochelle, France, fled to England in 1685, on the revocation of the Edict of Nantes. His son Augustus, for the same cause, emigrated to America, which has been the home of his descendants. He was the grandfather of John Jay, LL.D., a patriot of the American Revolution and the early days of the Republic. This talented and venerated statesman was graduated at Columbia College, New York. He was a leading member of the first Continental Congress, and was the author of the eloquent "Address to the People of Great Britain," of which Thomas Jefferson said that it was the production "of the finest pen in America." He was a prominent member of the New York Convention of 1776, and served on the most important committees. Mr. Jay was appointed Minister Plenipotentiary to Spain, and was one of the Commissioners to negotiate peace with Great Britain, signing the treaty of peace at Paris in 1783. On his return to New York he held the position of Secretary of Foreign Affairs for five years. In 1789, President Washington offered him the choice of any office in his power to bestow. He accepted that of Chief-Justice of the Supreme Court, which he resigned in 1794, to take the mission to England, where he succeeded in negotiating the treaty which bears his name. From 1795 to 1801 he was Governor of New York, and under his administration slavery was abolished in the State. From that time until his death, in 1829, he lived in the retirement of private life. His son, Judge William Jay, widely known as an author, jurist, and philanthropist, was the father of John Jay, the subject of this sketch.

The Honorable John Jay, late Envoy Extraordinary and Minister Plenipotentiary to Austria, was born in New York City, June 23, 1817. His education was commenced under private tutors, and was continued at Muhlenbergh's Institute, Flushing, and at Columbia College, New York, where he graduated at the age of nineteen, ranking second in his class. He then read law in the office of the late Daniel Lord, Jr., and was admitted to the bar in 1839.

In 1834, while pursuing his studies at college, young Mr. Jay became a manager of the New York Young Men's Anti-Slavery Society. The decided stand thus early taken, regarding the long and much-discussed question of Abolition, was steadfastly maintained to the time when it became a matter of vital importance to the Union. Throughout the great struggle which resulted in favor of the cause which he supported, Mr. Jay was opposed to the annexation of Texas, and to the admission to the Union of any slave-owning territories. He also defended, in the New York courts, during several years, persons arrested as fugitive slaves.

During the Civil War, Mr. Jay was associated first with the Loyal National League of New York, which had numerous branches throughout the State, and also with the Union League Club. He was a manager of the Freedman's Aid Society of New York. In 1865 he assisted in accomplishing a union of all the Aid Societies of the North and West, and took part in the inauguration of the Freedman's Aid Union at Cooper Institute. During the war of the rebellion he advocated the enlistment of colored men, a Proclamation of Emancipation, the organization of a Freedman's Bureau, and the adoption by Congress of the Constitutional Amendment abolishing slavery. In the autumn of that year he visited Europe for the second time. During his absence he was elected President of the Union League Club. This position he held until 1869, when President Grant appointed him Minister to Austria. He resigned this position in the autumn of 1874. In January, 1877, he was again elected to the Presidency of the Union League Club. In the following December he withdrew his name as a candidate for re-election. In April, 1877, he acted as chairman of a committee to investigate the New York Custom House. He has been for many years Manager and Corresponding Secretary of the New York Historical Society, as well as a member of several other societies. He is the author of numerous anti-slavery addresses and pamphlets; of pamphlets on subjects connected with the Protestant Episcopal Church; and has published legal arguments, political addresses, reports, etc. In October, 1878, he delivered an eloquent address on "The Value of the Bible as a National Defense," before the Westchester County Bible Society, of which his father and his grandfather each in succession long held the position of President. The latter was also one of the earlier Presidents of the American Bible Society.

FREDERICK WILLIAM VON STEUBEN.

Frederick William Augustus Henry Ferdinand von Steuben was born November 15, 1730, at Magdeburg, in Prussia. He was educated in the Jesuit colleges at Neisse and Breslau, where he applied himself particularly to mathematics. At the age of seventeen he became a cadet in an infantry regiment, and by the time he attained his twenty-fifth year he had become a first lieutenant. In 1757 he distinguished himself in the battles of Prague and Rosbach, and the following year entered as Adjutant-General the free corps of General von Mayr. In 1762 he was appointed Adjutant-General on the personal staff of Frederick the Great, " in whose suite he took part in the celebrated siege of Schweidnitz, the surrender of which was the brilliant conclusion of the military operations of the Seven Years' War." After the close of this struggle the Prussian king presented him with a valuable lay benefice of the religious chapter of Havelsburg. He was also admitted to the select circle of young officers to whom Frederick in person gave special instructions in the art of war. After the close of the war Steuben travelled in Europe with the Prince of Hohenzollern Hechingen, in whose court he discharged the duties of grand marshal and general of his body-guard for ten years. He afterwards withdrew to the court of the Margrave of Baden, who had previously decorated him with the Order of Fidelity. While in the service of this Prince he received the commission of Lieutenant-General.

In 1777 Baron von Steuben, while on his way to England, stopped at Paris, where he met an acquaintance, the Count St. Germain, then holding the high position of Minister of War. The count induced him to go to America, then deep in her struggle for liberty. After a long, and more than ordinarily perilous voyage, the ship on which he embarked arrived at Portsmouth, New Hampshire, on the 1st of December. He immediately addressed letters to Congress and to General Washington, inclosing copies of letters of introduction from Benjamin Franklin, and tendering his services as a volunteer in the patriot army. He was promptly commissioned by Congress to join the army under Washington, at Valley Forge. This winter was one of great hardship and suffering to the Continental troops. They were very inadequately provided for in many respects, and were sadly in need of military instruction. General Washington conferred upon Baron Steuben the temporary appointment of Inspector-General, and he immediately entered upon his work of disciplining the recruits. In May, 1778, his appointment was confirmed by Congress. He fought as a volunteer at the battle of Monmouth, in the following June, and rendered important services throughout the war.

In 1779 Steuben prepared a manual of military drill and tactics, entitled "Regulations for the Order and Discipline of the Troops of the United States." This work received the approval of Washington, and was adopted by Congress. "Seldom has a book been composed under similar circumstances. Each chapter was at first roughly written in German, then translated into bad French, then put in good French by Fleury, translated again into bad English by Duponceau, afterwards written in good English by Captain Walker; and when all this was completed, Steuben himself did not understand one word of it in consequence of his ignorance of the English language."

In 1780 Baron Steuben was appointed a member of a board of general officers for the trial of Major André. At the close of the war he was sent to Canada by Washington, commissioned to demand of General Haldiman the delivery of the frontier posts of the territory ceded to the United States. Upon his return he was instructed to disband the military posts at Philadelphia, and in November, in company with General Washington, entered the city of New York upon its evacuation by the British. In 1784 he tendered his resignation to Congress. It was accepted, and at the same time a resolution was passed voting him a gold-hilted sword. In 1790 Congress voted him a life annuity of two thousand five hundred dollars. Several of the States had previously passed resolutions acknowledging his numerous and valuable services to the country, and also voting him tracts of land. New York presented him with sixteen thousand acres, near the present city of Utica, forming a township called from him Steuben. The latter years of his life were passed on this estate and in the city of New York, where he was a prominent member of the most distinguished society of the day. He was President of the German Society, and President of the New York State Society of the Cincinnati.

Baron von Steuben died at his home in Steubenville, New York, November 28, 1794. His remains were interred at a hillside within his own domains.

STEPHEN ARNOLD DOUGLAS.

STEPHEN ARNOLD DOUGLAS was born in Brandon, Rutland County, Vermont, April 23, 1813. The family is of Scotch descent. His grandfather was a soldier of the American Revolution, and was with Washington at Valley Forge and Yorktown. His father, a skillful and trusted physician, died suddenly of heart disease, while holding his two months' old son, the future statesman, in his arms.

Until he reached the age of fifteen years, Stephen A. Douglas, who was an apt and persevering scholar, studied at the common schools of his native State. If the necessary means had been his, he would have entered College; but as they were not, he relinquished the thought of a more thorough education, to commence earning his own living. He apprenticed himself to a cabinet-maker, and worked at that trade for eighteen months, when his health becoming impaired he resumed his studies. Choosing the law as a profession, he prepared for it at the same time that he pursued his academic course. In the spring of 1833 he went west, and finally settled in Jacksonville, Illinois. He taught school for a while, devoting all the time he could secure to his legal studies. He was admitted to the bar in 1834, and soon obtained a lucrative practice. Before a year had passed, though he had not yet attained his twenty-second year, he was elected Attorney-General of the State. In 1837 he was appointed by President Van Buren, Register of the Land Office at Springville, and the same year was a Democratic candidate for Congress. In 1840 he was appointed Secretary of the State of Illinois, and in 1841 was elected a Judge of the Supreme Court. He performed his duties as Judge with acknowledged ability. In 1842 he received the nomination for Congress, and was elected. He was re-elected in 1844 and in 1846; but after the last election, and before the commencement of his term, he was elected a Senator of the United States for the term ending in 1853. He was twice re-elected to the Senate, his duties in that body terminating only with his life. In his long Congressional career, he generally adopted the principles and advocated the policy of the Democratic party. He was prominent in the Oregon controversy, and was one of the last to surrender. He was also a supporter of the annexation of Texas. He was a firm advocate of the extension of the 36° 30' line to the Pacific ocean, and voted against the Wilmot Proviso. In 1854 he brought forward his famous bill organizing the Territories of Kansas and Nebraska, and advocating the doctrine of "Squatter sovereignty," *i. e.*, the right of the inhabitants of each Territory to decide for themselves whether each State should come into the Union a slave or free State. Though this was in fact a repeal of the Missouri Compromise, and throughout the discussion great bitterness of feeling prevailed, he carried his measure through Congress in spite of all opposition.

In 1856 Mr. Douglas was a Democratic candidate for the presidential nomination. Buchanan received the nomination, and Douglas supported him in the ensuing campaign. In 1857 the Lecompton controversy arose. Mr. Douglas thought that, under a strict adherence to the Democratic faith, Congress ought not to accept a constitution unless it was the act of the people. In promoting the local interests of Illinois he was remarkably successful. The construction of the Illinois Central Railroad was due principally to him. He strongly advocated the construction of a railroad from the Mississippi river to the Pacific ocean. In foreign policy he opposed the treaty with England limiting the Oregon Territory to the 49th parallel. He also opposed the ratification of the Clayton-Bulwer treaty. He favored the acquisition of Cuba whenever that island could be obtained consistently with the laws of nations and the honor of the United States.

In 1860 Mr. Douglas was the candidate of the Democratic party of the North for the presidency. There were three other candidates in the field, the representatives of as many political parties. John C. Breckinridge was the candidate of the Democratic party of the South, John Bell of the Union party, and Abraham Lincoln of the Republican party. Of the elective popular vote of more than four millions and a half, Mr. Douglas received over one million three hundred thousand, within about five hundred thousand of the vote of Mr. Lincoln. During the stormy time which followed the election, Mr. Douglas raised his voice in the Senate in behalf of the Union, and continued to support and defend it until his death, which took place in Chicago, June 3, 1861. Mr. Douglas was one of the most remarkable men in the public service of the United States. He was a powerful speaker, and possessed great personal influence with the masses. His small stature— he was somewhat below the middle height—procured him the title of "The Little Giant," by which he was popularly known.

GEORGE WASHINGTON BETHUNE.

George W. Bethune, D.D., the wit, poet and preacher, was born in New York City, March 18, 1805. He traced his family descent to the Huguenots. His father, Divie Bethune, was a prominent citizen of New York. Before a Tract Society was formed in this country, he printed ten thousand tracts at his own expense, and distributed many of them himself. This circumstance led Dr. Bethune to remark that he was "the son of the first American Tract Society!" Dr. Bethune's maternal grandmother was the distinguished Christian, and accomplished woman, Isabella Graham.

Dr. Bethune received a liberal education. He spent three years at Columbia College, was graduated at Dickinson College in 1822, and at Princeton Theological Seminary in 1825. In 1826 he was ordained a Presbyterian minister, but the following year joined the Dutch Reformed Church. His first ministerial charge was at Rhinebeck, on the Hudson, from whence he removed to Utica; and in 1834, to Philadelphia, where he was connected with two churches. In 1849 he was called to Brooklyn, where for ten years he continued at the head of a large congregation. His church edifice was handsome, and was remarkable for receiving light from "above," which produced a pleasing effect.

In 1859 Dr. Bethune's impaired health led him to resign his charge of the Brooklyn church, and cross the ocean for rest and restoration. He visited Italy, and preached for a time at the American Chapel at Rome. In 1860 he returned to New York, and became associate pastor of a church in that city, but his continued ill-health soon compelled him to return to Italy. After a few months' residence at Florence, he died at that place, April 27, 1862.

Dr. Bethune was the author of several works, written more for his own people than for the public, but which attained a large circulation. Among them are, "The Fruits of the Spirit," "Early Lost," "Early

Saved," and "The History of a Penitent," all popular works of a devotional character. In 1847 he edited the first American edition of Walton's "Angler," a work which he performed in the careful and agreeable manner befitting his own reputation as an enthusiastic and highly celebrated follower of the "contemplative man's recreation," and as an accomplished scholar.

Dr. Bethune was a pleasing poet. In 1848 he published "Lays of Love and Faith, and other Poems." In 1850 he published a volume of "Orations and Occasional Discourses." The volume comprises funeral discourses on the death of Stephen Van Rensselaer, the Patroon of Albany, N. Y., President Harrison, and General Jackson; lectures and college addresses upon "Genius," "Leisure, its Uses and Abuses," "Age of Pericles," "Prospect of Art in the United States," "Eloquence of the Pulpit," "Duties of Educated Men," "A Plea for Study," and "The Claims of our Country upon its Literary Men." He also collected and published a portion of his Sermons. In 1864 a collection of his sermons in two volumes was published by Sheldon & Company, New York. They were entitled, "Expository Lectures on the Heidelberg Catechism," a subject upon which he had bestowed much attention. In 1867 the same firm also published the "Memoir of Rev. George W. Bethune, D.D.," written by Rev. A. R. Van Nest.

Dr. Bethune was a careful preacher, though far from being formal and precise in the arrangement of sentences, or in their delivery. On the contrary, his sermons were peculiar for their simple ease, grace, and perfect finish. "The enlightened were attracted by comprehensiveness of thought, and the refined by care in elaboration, while the uncultured enjoyed their simplicity and were impressed by their earnestness."

Dr. Bethune possessed a social disposition, and was a great favorite with all who became associated with him either on public occasions or in private life. He was a genial conversationalist, and from his well-stored memory he drew many a pathetic or humorous anecdote for the entertainment and amusement of his friends. His fine humor and off-hand extempore speaking made him a valued acquisition at society meetings. He was a thorough and cultured scholar and possessed a large library, and the appearance of his study reminded one of Dickens's description of fog in London—" books on the walls, books to the ceiling, books in the closet, books in the recess, books on the tables, books on the floor, books on books, books everywhere."

THEODORE WINTHROP.

Major Theodore Winthrop, U. S. V., was born in New Haven, Connecticut, September 21, 1828, and was a lineal descendant of the first John Winthrop, who conducted from England one of the noblest of the many bands of Puritan colonists, and eventually became Governor of the Commonwealth of Massachusetts. His mother was a granddaughter of President Dwight, and a sister of President Woolsey. Thus the mere name of Winthrop is suggestive of New England memories and virtues. Theodore Winthrop entered Yale College from a well-known New Haven school, and was graduated with honor in the class of 1848. Soon after graduation, Winthrop and others constituted the first class in the "School of Philosophy and Arts," a department established during the previous year. Close application his studies proved too much for his health, and his physicians prescribed travel. He embarked in July, 1849, for Europe, where he spent more than a year.

In April, 1851, three months after his return from abroad, Mr. Winthrop joined the Pacific Mail Steamship Company, at the invitation of Mr. W. H. Aspinwall, whose acquaintance he had made in Europe. In the fall of 1852 he went to Panama, and spent the two following years on the Isthmus in the employment of the company. He also visited California, Oregon, and Vancouver's Island, and accompanied the unfortunate expedition of Lieutenant Strain to explore the Isthmus of Darien.

Upon his return to New York Mr. Winthrop studied law in the office of Charles Tracey, and after his admission to the bar remained with him as a clerk for another year. Going to St. Louis he practised law for a time; but the climate and mode of life not proving congenial, he returned in the summer of 1858, to discover at length his true calling—the field of literature and authorship. His first appearance in print was as the author of a description of the famous landscape, "The Heart of the Andes," by Frederic Edwin Church. "An intimate friend of the artist, he sat by the easel and saw the picture as it grew to completeness under his rapid but sure touch, and the work so warmed his brain that he sought utterance for his admiration in words as glowing as the tropic sunshine of the picture."

Immediately after the fall of Fort Sumter, in April, 1861, Winthrop dropped the pen and grasped the sword. He joined the Seventh Regiment at New York, marched with it to Washington, sharing the hardships and fatigue of the way; became, at Fortress Monroe, a member of General Butler's staff, as aid and military secretary, with the rank of Major. He aided in planning the attack on the batteries of Great Bethel, where, on the disastrous 10th of June, 1861, he fell while waving his sword at the front, and cheering his comrades to the charge. His courage and bearing throughout the fight had rendered him especially conspicuous, and elicited the admiration of both friends and foes. His remains were brought to New York. The funeral services were conducted at the armory of the Seventh Regiment, and the body was carried through Broadway on the howitzer which he had helped to drag, only two months before, through the same thoroughfare.

When Mr. Winthrop left New York for the seat of war, he was engaged to write a series of sketches, to be entitled "The March of the Seventh," for the "Atlantic Monthly." He left at his death a number of unpublished manuscripts, which were soon given to the public. "Cecil Dreeme" was published soon after his decease, and at once attracted much attention. The scenes of this story are, for the most part, laid in the studios of the New York University.

"John Brent" was next published. "This novel carries us across the Plains from California in a style such as pen has never crossed them before. The book should have been called 'Don Fulano,' in honor of the matchless steed which so faithfully bears his master to the redressal of wrong and setting up of right, at an eventful crisis. A horse has seldom been so admirably described, so sharply individualized. It is a work to rank with the great masters of the chisel and the palette as well as of the pen. The descriptions of prairie life, of the mountain-passes, the wavy landscape, the far-off approach of caravans, are admirable."

Many of Mr. Winthrop's other writings soon found their way into print. Among them were "Edwin Brothertoft," a novel; and two volumes of travelling sketches, "The Canoe and the Saddle," and "Life in the Open Air."

BENJAMIN WEST, P.R.A.

Benj. West

BENJAMIN WEST.

Benjamin West, one of the earliest American painters, was born near Springfield, Pennsylvania, October 10, 1738. His parents, who were Quakers, allowed him to cultivate his talent for drawing and painting, though such a course was in opposition to the rigid principles of their sect. He began to make drawings from nature in his seventh year, and a year or so later he received a present of a paint-box, which was to him an inspiration. "Even after going to sleep he awoke more than once during the night and anxiously put out his hand to the box, which he had placed by his bedside, half afraid that he might find his riches only a dream. Next morning he rose at break of day, and carrying his colors and canvas to the garret, proceeded to work. Everything else was now unheeded; even his attendance at school was given up. As soon as he got out of the sight of his father and mother he stole to his garret, and here passed the hours in a world of his own. At last, after he had been absent from school some days, the master called at his father's house to inquire what had become of him. This led to the discovery of his secret occupation. His mother, proceeding to the garret, found the truant; but so much was she astonished and delighted by the creation of his pencil, which also met her view when she entered the apartment, that, instead of rebuking him, she could only take him in her arms, and kiss him with transports of affection. He made a new composition of his own out of two engravings, which he had colored from his own feeling of the proper tints, and so perfect did the performance already appear to his mother, that although half the canvas yet remained uncovered, she would not suffer him to add another touch to what he had done. Mr. Galt, West's biographer, saw the picture in the state in which it had thus been left, sixty-seven years afterwards, and the artist himself used to acknowledge that in none of his subsequent efforts had he been able to excel some of the touches of invention in this his first essay."

BENJAMIN WEST.

In 1756 young West went to Philadelphia, where he received such elementary instruction in his art as that city then afforded. He established himself there as a portrait-painter, and subsequently went to New York, where he continued to practise his profession or art. In 1760 he was enabled to visit Italy, where his portrait of Lord Grantham, at first generally attributed to Raphael Mengs, excited much interest. In 1763 he went to England on his way to America, but he met with such encouragement there that he took up his permanent residence in London. He died in that city, March 11, 1820, and was buried in St. Paul's. For many years he enjoyed the favor and patronage of the King. He was happy in his domestic and social relations, and was blessed with ample means and a wide spread reputation. "When we connect in fancy West's humble birthplace with his cathedral tomb, and revive the details of his life, we recognize a singular exception to the fortunes of our early native artists, most of whom had so long a conflict with adverse circumstances. Indeed, the comfort he enjoyed may somewhat account for the absence of intensity and aspiration in his genius; spirituality is the offspring of deep experience; he suffered no trying ordeal, he was not disciplined and elevated by the battle of life: his success was too easily achieved; order, calmness, and regularity marked his experience not less than his character. It is an anomalous fact in American artist-life that our earliest painter was the most prosperous."

During the last forty years of his life Mr. West sketched or painted at least four hundred pictures, most of them large, and left two hundred elaborate drawings. In 1762 he succeeded Sir Joshua Reynolds as president of the Royal Academy, and he was holding that office at the time of his death. "One of his early pictures, the 'Death of Wolfe,' widely known through the fine engravings of Wollett, may be said to have created an era in the history of British art, from the fact that the figures were habited in the costume appropriate to their time and character." He painted for George III. a number of subjects taken from early English history. The first of a series of religious pieces, "Christ Healing the Sick," was intended as a present to the Pennsylvania Hospital in Philadelphia, but it was purchased for £3,000 by the British Institute, and he afterward sent a copy with some alterations to Philadelphia. His "Death on the Pale Horse" is in the Philadelphia Academy of Fine Arts. In the opinion of many, his "Christ Rejected" is his best picture in America. Among those in England, the "Pylades and Orestes" is one of the best.

ROGER BROOKE TANEY.

ROGER BROOKE TANEY, the celebrated American jurist, was born in Calvert County, Maryland, March 17, 1777. He was graduated from Dickinson College, Pennsylvania, in 1795. Four years later he completed his legal studies and was admitted to the bar. He had scarcely commenced the practice of his profession in his native county, when he was elected a member of the House of Delegates as a Federalist. In 1801 he removed to Frederick, where he resided for the next twenty years.

In 1816 Mr. Taney was elected to the State Senate. In 1822 he removed to Baltimore, where he continued to reside until his death. Devoting himself to the law, he secured an extensive practice in the State and Federal Courts, still finding time, however, to watch with interest the political movements of the times, even when not participating in them. Though originally a Federalist, he eventually identified himself with the supporters of General Jackson. This, however, did not prevent his appointment in 1827 as Attorney-General of the State by the Federal Governor.

In 1831 President Jackson appointed him Attorney-General of the United States. In this office he supported the President in the course he pursued with regard to the bill renewing the charter of the United States Bank. In 1833 he was appointed Secretary of the Treasury, to fill the place of Mr. Duane, who had been dismissed from that office. He at once issued orders for the removal of the Government deposits from the United States Bank to local banks. When his nomination was communicated to the Senate that body rejected it. This was also the case with his nomination as a Justice of the Supreme Court in 1835. Upon the death of Chief-Justice Marshall the President nominated Mr. Taney as his successor, and he took his seat in January, 1837.

As a judge Mr. Taney showed great ability. The most noted of his decisions was that in the celebrated "Dred Scott" case. "In that case Scott, who was held as a slave in Missouri, brought suit to recover his freedom, suing in the Federal Court on the ground of being a citizen of a different State from the defendant, and claiming his freedom from having been taken by his master into territory made free by the Act of Congress commonly called the Missouri Compromise. The case having been decided in the Circuit Court, was removed to the Supreme Court. The decision (1857) declared that Scott was not entitled to bring suit in the Federal Court, because he was not a citizen; the Chief-Justice, in an elaborate opinion, declaring that for more than a century previous to the adoption of the Declaration of Independence negroes, whether slave or free, had been regarded 'as beings of an inferior order, and altogether unfit to associate with the white race, either in social or political relations, and so far inferior that they had no rights which the white man was bound to respect.' Having reached this conclusion, which of itself put an end to the case, the court went further, and considered the main question involved, namely, whether it was competent for Congress to exclude slavery from the territories of the Union; and the majority, Justices McLean and Curtis dissenting, denied the power. The party, dissatisfied with this conclusion, made it the occasion for a severe arraignment of the court, not only because of the views held as to the right to legislate against slavery, but because those views were expressed in a case not calling for them, inasmuch as the court had already decided that it had no jurisdiction. The decision, in its denial of the right of citizenship to negroes, was disregarded by the executive department after Mr. Lincoln became President, and by the judicial also when Mr. Chase became Chief-Justice, and admitted colored persons as practitioners in the Federal Courts."

Chief-Justice Taney died in Washington, D. C., October 12, 1864. A bronze statute of him by Rinehart, ordered by the State of Maryland, was unveiled at Annapolis, December 10, 1872.

FRANCIS WAYLAND.

Francis Wayland was born in New York, March 11, 1796. His parents were characterized by integrity, industry, common sense, strong religious convictions, and ardent love for civil and religious liberty. The son was not, as a boy, distinguished for brilliancy, but was sturdy, reliable, and brave. In the schools which he attended in his childhood, there was no thought of teaching; the scholar committed to memory, whether he understood or not. Young Wayland could recite page after page of Lowth's Grammar, and could repeat the boundaries of the countries, but had no idea what it was all about. When he was ten years old, the family removed to Poughkeepsie, and the lad came under the instruction of Mr. Daniel H. Barnes, a real teacher, for whose conscientious thoroughness he was always grateful. In 1811, he entered Union College at an advanced standing, and graduated in 1813. He studied medicine for three years. Meanwhile, his views of life and of religious duty changed; he became a member of the Baptist Church, and resolved to devote himself to the Christian ministry. He spent a year at Andover Theological Seminary, chiefly under the instruction of Professor Moses Stuart, the pioneer of exegetical study in America. His scanty means being exhausted, he became a tutor in Union College. The four years which he spent in this position brought him into close contact with the sage Dr. Nott, whose counsels were of measureless value to the young man.

In 1821, Mr. Wayland became pastor of the First Baptist Church in Boston. The church was weak, and the house badly located; but the life-long maxim of Wayland held good: "Nothing will stand before days' works." He grew in power; his sermon on "The Moral Dignity of the Missionary Enterprise" (1823), made him known wherever the English language was spoken.

In 1827, he became President of Brown University, entering on what was to be the work of his life. The University was poor; library, cabinet, and apparatus scarcely existed; discipline and scholarship were little more than a name. The new President sought to make the college as good as possible. He replaced routine by life and freshness; in the class-room he encouraged inquiry and discussion; he laid aside the antiquated text-books, and taught by lectures, till in his several studies he had created new treatises. It was remarked at the bar and in the pulpit that a graduate of "Brown" could be known by his closeness of reasoning and his power of analysis. The funds were enlarged; apparatus, cabinet, and library were created, and buildings were erected for them. Still the President was not satisfied. The university (in common with all American colleges) was not fulfilling its destiny. It was offering an education suited only to the learned professions, and it was ignoring the boundless diversity of aim and intellectual character on the part of the students. The college was reorganized on the basis suggested by the President. The step resulted very successfully, enlarging the number of students, and widely extending the benefits of education. The changes introduced in the American colleges since 1850 have all been in the direction which he pointed out.

His efforts for the moral and religious welfare of his pupils were unceasing. His sermons, his counsels, his personal appeals, combined with his strong power of sympathy, and the power of his own example, exerted a life-long transforming and elevating influence. His labors outside the college were arduous and untiring, touching all that related to the welfare of the city, State, and nation, to the progress of education and religion. He published eighteen volumes, besides more than fifty discourses, sermons, and addresses. His "Moral Science" had a circulation of more than 150,000. It has been republished in England and in Scotland, and translated into Armenian, Modern Greek, Hawaiian, and Nestorian.

These varied labors weighed heavily upon him, and in 1855 he resigned his position as President. His remaining days were devoted to humane and religious labor, to reading, study, and authorship, and to the cultivation of his garden, which had been his one recreation, passion, and luxury. He closed a life devoted to the service of God and the welfare of man, at his home in Providence, R. I., Sept. 30, 1865, in his 70th year.

The leading feature of his character and the source of his success was his unwavering and conscientious devotion to duty. In the words of a pupil and successor (President Robinson), "To him 'ought' and 'ought not' were the most powerful words that could be spoken."

Edmund Pendleton Gaines

EDMUND PENDLETON GAINES.

MAJOR-GENERAL EDMUND PENDLETON GAINES, U. S. A., was born in Culpepper County, Virginia, March 20, 1777. His father, James Gaines, commanded a company in the Revolutionary War, and was subsequently in the North Carolina Legislature, and in the Convention which ratified the Federal Constitution. He was the nephew of Edmund Pendleton—after whom the son was named—a profound and able lawyer and judge of Virginia.

In the sparsely settled region in which the early boyhood of Edmund P. Gaines was spent, educational advantages were few. All opportunities were improved under the direction and encouragement of his mother, who was intelligent and well informed. An early friend taught him so much of the elements of mathematics as to make him an accurate surveyor. When he was about thirteen years of age his father removed his family to Sullivan County, which afterwards became the Eastern County of Tennessee. Young Gaines had early been taught to labor, to swing the axe and follow the plough. In his hours of pastime he rambled through the forests in search of game, his rifle his constant companion, and he is said to have excelled in the use of that weapon. He was scarcely above the ordinary height, and slight of person, but straight as the arrow of an Indian warrior. His constitution, naturally strong and vigorous, had become hardened and invigorated, and fitted to endure the sufferings and vicissitudes of a soldier's life. His leisure hours were spent in reading and studying such military and historical works as he could procure. At the age of eighteen he was elected to a lieutenancy in a rifle company.

When the young man became legally of age, he commenced the study of law, and pursued it as rapidly as his limited means would allow. While thus engaged, he was recommended by the Hon. W. C C. Claiborne, then a Member of Congress, for an appointment in the army, and January 10, 1799, received his first commission, as ensign. In the fall of that year he was promoted to the rank of second lieutenant in the Sixth Infantry, and sent on the recruiting service. From 1801 to the winter of 1803-4, he was engaged in making a topographical survey from Nashville to Natchez, for the location of a military road, and in the survey of some Indian boundary lines. In the meantime he had become a first lieutenant.

In 1804 he was appointed military collector for the district of Mobile. Two years later he received the appointment of post-master, and was selected as the confidential agent of the post-office department, with the power of suspending post-masters and contractors concerned in what was called "The Conspiracy of Aaron Burr." He was active in the mission entrusted to him, and arrested Colonel Burr. After the close of the trial he practised law for a time, but when war was declared against Great Britain he resumed his position in the army. He had some years before risen to the rank of captain. In the war which followed he soon became distinguished among the most steadfast in the faithful performance of every arduous duty. The post of greatest danger was to him the post of honor. There he was always to be found. In March, 1812, he became major of the Eighth Infantry; in July, lieutenant-colonel of the Twenty-fourth Infantry; in March, 1813, colonel of the Twenty-fifth Infantry, and in September, adjutant-general with the rank of colonel. He took part in the battle of Chrystler's Field, November 11, and in that action commanded the Twenty-fifth Infantry, one of the finest and most effective regiments in the service. In March, 1814, he received the commission of a brigadier-general. For his gallantry at Fort Erie, where he was severely wounded, August 28, he was brevetted a major-general. This was the highest rank authorized by law. The Government also honored him with a unanimous vote of thanks, and authorized the President to present to him a gold medal. Similar votes of thanks were passed, and gold-hilted swords presented to him by the Legislatures of New York, Virginia, and Tennessee.

General Gaines served under General Jackson in the Creek War, and for several years was engaged in like service. He was severely wounded in an action with the Seminole Indians in February, 1836. At the breaking out of the Mexican War he was thought to have exceeded his authority in calling out a large number of the Southern militia, and sending them to the seat of war. For this he was tried by a court-martial in July, 1845, but was not censured. Soon after he was assigned to the command of the eastern division, and at the close of the war with Mexico was relieved from duty at his own request.

General Gaines died in New Orleans, June 6, 1849.

EDWARDS PIERREPONT.

The Hon. Edwards Pierrepont was born in New Haven, Connecticut, in the year 1817. He is a descendant of the Reverend James Pierrepont, the second minister of New Haven and one of the founders of Yale College. This family was allied to the noble English race of that name which held the earldom of Kingston.

Edwards Pierrepont studied at the Hopkins Grammar School of his native city, and was graduated at Yale College, in the class of 1837, with high honors. Chief-Justice Waite and Secretary Evarts were his classmates. His legal education was received at the New Haven Law School, under Judge Daggett and Judge Hitchcock. In 1840 he commenced the practice of his profession in Columbus, Ohio. In January, 1846, he removed to the city of New York, where he has since resided, and where he has for many years been eminent at the bar. In 1857 he was elected a Judge of the Superior Court of New York, to fill a vacancy caused by the death of Chief-Justice Oakley. In 1860 he resigned his seat upon the bench and resumed the practice of the law. Until the breaking out of the War of the Rebellion he had always been a Democrat. He then became a member of the Union Defence Company, and was a zealous supporter of the administration of Abraham Lincoln, who, in 1862, appointed him, with General Dix, to try the prisoners of state then confined in the various prisons and forts of the United States. In 1867 he was elected a member of the convention for forming a new constitution for the State of New York, and one of the Judiciary Committee. In the spring of the same year he was employed to conduct the prosecution, on the part of the Government, of John H. Surratt, indicted for complicity in the murder of President Lincoln. This celebrated trial commenced before the United States District Court in the city of Washington on the 6th of June, 1867, and lasted until the 10th of the next August.

In the Presidential contests of 1868 and 1872, Judge Pierrepont was a warm supporter of General Grant, and made numerous public speeches on the Republican side. Upon his accession to the Presidency, in 1869, General Grant appointed Judge Pierrepont Attorney of the United States for the Southern District of New York, which office he resigned in July, 1870. In the autumn of 1870 he was one of the most active of the "Committee of Seventy" against the "Ring Frauds" of New York.

Judge Pierrepont received the degree of LL.D. from Columbia College, Washington, June, 1871, having in that year delivered an oration before the graduating class of the Law School of that institution. In 1873 he received the same degree from Yale College. In May of that year he was offered the position of American Minister at the Russian Court, which honor he declined. In 1875 he was appointed Attorney-General of the United States. While Attorney-General he argued many important causes on the part of the Government, among which were the noted Union Pacific Railway case and the Arkansas Hot Springs case. He was also called upon by the Secretary of State to prepare an opinion upon a great question of international law, which gave him a wide reputation in Europe. He remained in the Cabinet of President Grant until May, 1876, when he was appointed Envoy Extraordinary and Minister Plenipotentiary at the Court of St. James.

In 1877, the second year of his mission at the Court of St. James, ex-President Grant visited Great Britain. "Mr. Pierrepont was well aware of the importance there attached to title, rank, and the forms of precedence; and when quite a young man had felt much chagrin in London that two ex-Presidents of the United States had been received in that capital only as respectable private gentlemen, while the ex-rulers of other countries were received with great distinction and accorded marked precedence. He insisted that in England, where forms are substance and where precedence is evidence of respect, that to refuse such evidence to a great power like the United States, and at the same time to accord it to every deposed prince of a petty kingdom, indicated, whether so intended or not, a want of due respect towards our form of government. The Queen's ministers acted with the utmost delicacy and friendliness in the matter, and ex-President Grant was received with the highest distinctions. The example of England was followed by other European governments."

Mr. Pierrepont also negotiated with Lord Derby, the British Minister of Foreign Affairs, the Trade-mark Treaty. He resigned his office at the end of 1877. The University of Oxford conferred upon him the degree of D.C.L., the highest honor in its gift.

DAVID HUNTER.

DAVID HUNTER, Major-General of Volunteers and Brevet Major-General of the regular Army of the United States, was born in the city of Washington, District of Columbia, July 21, 1802. Entering the West Point Military Academy at the age of sixteen, he graduated in 1822, the twenty-fifth in rank in a class of forty, and on the 1st of July received the appointment of second lieutenant in the Fifth Regiment of the United States Infantry. In 1828 he was promoted to the rank of first lieutenant, and in 1833 to a captaincy in the First Dragoons, in which capacity he twice crossed the plains to the Rocky Mountains. He resigned his position in the army in 1836, and entered the forwarding business in Chicago. He, however, returned to the army in 1841 as paymaster, with the rank of major, which rank he held at the time of the breaking out of the civil war in 1861.

Major Hunter was one of the four officers detailed by the War Department to escort the newly-elected President from Springfield to Washington; but at Buffalo, owing to the pressure of the crowd, he suffered a dislocation of the collar-bone. Shortly after, May 14, 1861, he was commissioned colonel of the Sixth United States Cavalry. At the battle of Bull Run he commanded the second division, but was severely wounded in the neck early in the action, and compelled to return to Washington.

On the 3d of August, 1861, Colonel Hunter was appointed a brigadier-general of volunteers, his commission to bear date May 17, 1861; and on the 13th of August he was made a major-general of volunteers, and sent to Missouri as second in command. On the 27th of October General Fremont arrived at Springfield, and was preparing to attack Price, when, on the 2d of November, he received a peremptory order to turn over the command to General Hunter, who arrived on the following day and formally assumed the command.

On the 19th of November, 1861, General Halleck formally assumed command of the Western Department, and General Hunter was assigned to the Department of Kansas, where he remained until March, 1862. On the 15th of that month he was ordered to the Department of the South, with headquarters at Hilton Head, Port Royal, South Carolina. He arrived there on the 30th, and immediately assumed command. One of his first and most important acts was the issue of a proclamation declaring slavery abolished in his department. He also organized a negro brigade, and detailed officers to train them to the use of arms. Both willing and able, they soon attained considerable proficiency, and under the wise administration of General Saxton did good service in the cause of liberty.

The Confederate Congress at Richmond immediately passed resolutions to hang General Hunter, and also General Phelps, who had issued a similar order, if captured, instead of treating them as prisoners of war. The President annulled General Hunter's order on the 19th of May, 1862, and compelled General Phelps to resign and come home.

Early in September, 1862, General Hunter was ordered to Washington to act as president of a court of inquiry on the surrender of Harper's Ferry, McClellan's Maryland campaign, etc., and as president of a number of courts-martial. On the decease of Major-General Mitchel, November 30, 1862, General Hunter was reappointed to the command of the Department of the South, but was retained in Washington by the above-mentioned court.

General Hunter commanded the Department of West Virginia from May 19 to August 8, 1864. On June 5th, he met at Piedmont a Confederate force, under Major-General W. E. Jones, a cavalry officer of distinction. A spirited action resulted in the defeat and rout of the Confederates and the loss of their leader. During Hunter's march to Staunton, in the month of June, his men were engaged in several skirmishes with their foe. They took part in the action of Diamond Hill on the 17th, and of Lynchburg on the 18th. For these services he received the brevets of brigadier-general and of major-general of the United States Army.

In August, 1864, Major-General Philip Sheridan succeeded Major-General Hunter in command.

In July, 1866, General Hunter retired from the army.

CHARLES FORCE DEEMS.

CHARLES F. DEEMS, D.D., LL.D., pastor of the Church of the Strangers, New York City, was born in Baltimore, Maryland, December 4, 1820. He was graduated at Dickinson College, Pennsylvania, in 1839. During his senior year he was licensed to preach in the Methodist Church. At the age of twenty he was appointed General Agent of the American Bible Society for the State of North Carolina. He faithfully discharged the duties of that office until he resigned it in order to fill the chair of Logic and Rhetoric in the University of North Carolina. After five years of successful professorship he accepted the chair of Natural Science in Randolph Macon College, Virginia. He remained there but one year, however. In 1846 he was elected a delegate to the General Conference of the Methodist Episcopal Church, South, held in St. Louis, and was elected to the same position at every quadrennial session of that body until after his removal to New York. While in attendance at the Conference he was elected President of the Queensboro' Female College, in North Carolina. During the five years in which he held this position, he placed that institution on a permanent basis of prosperity. During this period Randolph Macon College conferred on him the degree of Doctor of Divinity. In 1854 he returned to the regular work of the ministry, and was appointed first to Goldsboro' and afterward to Front Street Church, Wilmington, in each of which places he remained two years. From 1858 to 1865 he was Presiding Elder of the Wilmington and Newbern districts. In December, 1865, he removed to the city of New York, where he edited a religious and literary weekly paper, which was published for a brief period. While thus engaged, he commenced preaching in the chapel of the University. Services were regularly held, and a new church organization was soon formed. There was insufficient room in the chapel for the accommodation of the large numbers who came to hear him, and a larger chapel in the same building was procured. The congregation became known as "The Church of the Strangers." It was intended "particularly for the benefit of the great number of persons who are temporarily in the city and desire to have a place for religious worship." In 1870, through the liberality of the late Commodore Vanderbilt, they secured the property belonging to the Mercer Street Presbyterian Church. Dr. Deems had the large and eligibly situated building rapidly repaired and fitted up, and on the 2d and 9th of October the dedicatory services were held. The church has constantly prospered, now numbers nearly six hundred members, and Dr. Deems probably preaches to the largest congregation, the year round, in the whole city, as the church is open every Sunday, and is generally filled and often overflowing.

In 1877 the degree of LL.D. was conferred on him by the University of North Carolina.

Dr. Deems is the author of from fifteen to twenty volumes on various subjects, and numerous published sermons. Among his works are "The Home Altar," which was translated into French; "What Now," a volume for young ladies; "Annals of Southern Methodism," a historical compilation of events, facts, and statistics connected with the church; and a small volume on practical religious subjects, entitled "Weights and Wings." Of his work entitled "Jesus," the learned Prof. Francis W. Upham, author of "The Wise Men," says: "I read, annotated, and carefully compared several Lives of Christ, that by Dr. Deems among them. Since then I have added to my list those of Farrar and Geikie, and still think now, as I did then, that his is the best of them all." He has also delivered addresses, speeches, and lectures. In addition to his other duties, he is editor of "The Sunday Magazine," published by Frank Leslie. He has been elected either President or Professor of nine colleges and universities.

Dr. Deems is below the medium height, though compact and well-proportioned. His deportment is at all times characterized by high-toned courtesy and genial warmth. Old and young are irresistibly attracted by him. He has fine conversational powers, and his natural talents, familiarity with ancient and modern literature, and extensive experience among all classes of men, render him an instructive and fascinating companion. "He has a vivid, spontaneous fancy, and at the same time his mind is naturally far-reaching, logical, and practical. Hence he is not only a thinker, but his thoughts weave themselves into the most chaste and beautiful language. He is impassioned even in argument; and there is in all that he writes and says the glow of earnest, sincere feeling. His thoughts are rapid and they are all aglow with sentiment and emotion, while they have a positiveness and interest which can only be imparted by extensive learning."

OLIVER PERRY MORTON.

OLIVER PERRY MORTON, a lawyer, senator, and prominent leader of the Republican party, was born in Wayne County, Indiana, August 4, 1823. His paternal grandfather was one of three brothers, who settled in New Jersey, in the days when the New World was constantly receiving acquisitions from the Old, in the form of energetic and enterprising men ready to labor for the furtherance of their own interests and those of a new and promising country. They were descended from the Earl of Throckmorton; but the Senator's father, when he became a Western pioneer, dropped the Throck, and afterward wrote his name William T. Morton. The mother of Oliver P. Morton, an intelligent and benevolent woman, died when he was quite young, and consequently his education was left to the care of others. During early boyhood he attended school through the winter months, and, as he grew older, worked at the hatters' trade. When he was fourteen years old, he was sent to a seminary in his native county, where General Lew. Wallace was among his schoolmates.

Young Morton was twenty years old when he entered Miami University at Oxford, Ohio, where he was a close student, and where he remained two years. After leaving college, he studied law, and in 1847, at the age of twenty-four, he was admitted to the bar, and opened an office in Centreville, Indiana. In ten years his practice had grown lucrative, and he was favorably known throughout that State and Ohio.

When Mr. Morton first took an interest in politics his sympathies were with the Democratic party. In 1852 he was elected Circuit Judge, but soon after retired from the bench, to return to his increasing practice. In 1854 the Missouri Compromise and the Kansas-Nebraska Bill were the means of adding him to the ranks of the Republican party. Two years later that party nominated him for Governor of his native State. He was defeated; but in 1860 he was nominated for Lieutenant-Governor, with Henry S. Lane for Governor. They were elected. When the Indiana Legislature convened early in

1861, Governor Lane was elected to the Senate of the United States, and Morton became Governor in his stead. He unquestionably rendered great service to the General Government during the war for the Union, and truly merited his name of "the great War Governor." The day before the President's call for troops, Governor Morton offered him ten thousand men. The Legislature voted and placed under his control five hundred thousand dollars for arms and ammunition, together with one hundred thousand dollars for military contingencies; they also voted a million dollars for enlisting and maintaining troops, and providing munitions of war. The whole history of the military operations of the State of Indiana during the war was highly honorable to the citizens of one of the most patriotic of the United States. Those who remained at home were unceasing in their efforts for the benefit of those who had gone forth to battle. Early in 1862 the State Sanitary Commission was organized, in accordance with the suggestions and plans of Governor Morton. The officers and agents of the Commission conducted the large and important business entrusted to them with great zeal and faithfulness.

When the armies on the Mississippi, and at Nashville, Tennessee, were suffering for lack of food, and the sick in the hospitals were almost destitute of proper supplies, the Governor dispatched boat after boat, laden with everything that could contribute to the comfort of the men. He established a Soldier's Home, and employed many additional surgeons to administer to the sick and wounded in the hospitals and in the field. In 1864 he was elected Governor for a second term. In 1865, having been stricken with paralysis, he visited Europe, with the hope that change of climate would benefit him. He was, however, from that time a cripple. He returned home in 1866, and entered into politics more actively than ever, in spite of his ill-health. In that year he was elected to the United States Senate for the term of 1867–'73, and upon its expiration was re-elected. Throughout his Senatorship he was known as the most radical of the leading Republicans. In 1870 President Grant nominated him Minister to England, but he declined. He served upon the Committees on Foreign Relations, Agriculture, Military Affairs, and Private Land Claims.

Senator Morton possessed a large and powerful frame, and it was a singular spectacle to see this strong man supported to his place in the Senate chamber. His most able speeches were made while seated in his chair at the National Capitol. He died at his home, in Indianapolis, Indiana, November 2, 1877.

ABRAM NEWKIRK LITTLEJOHN.

The Right Rev. A. N. Littlejohn, D.D., Bishop of the Diocese of Long Island, was born in Montgomery County, New York, December 13, 1824.

He was graduated at Union College in 1845, and was ordained a Deacon of the Episcopal Church in March, 1848. For nearly two years he officiated at St. Ann's church, Amsterdam, New York, and at St. Andrew's church, Meriden, Connecticut. In November, 1850, he was admitted to the priesthood, and about that time entered upon the rectorship of Christ church, Springfield, Massachusetts; but soon afterwards removed to St. Paul's church, New Haven. After a ministry there of more than nine years, he was called to the Church of the Holy Trinity, situated at the corner of Clinton and Montague Streets, in Brooklyn, New York, one of the largest and most important parishes of that "City of Churches."

After about eight years' ministry in this parish, during which time he endeared himself to his people, and was highly successful in promoting the prosperity of the church, he was elected Bishop of the newly created Diocese of Long Island, and consecrated, January 27, 1869. In the new field of labor to which he has been called, he is esteemed very efficient in the discharge of his duties, and is justly admired and beloved throughout his Diocese.

He has also, since July, 1874, had the charge of the American Episcopal churches on the continent of Europe.

In 1854, Dr. Littlejohn delivered, in Philadelphia, the first of a series of discourses by various bishops and clergymen on the "Evidences of Christianity." The series was subsequently published, with an able introduction by Bishop Potter, of Pennsylvania. For several years he performed the duties of lecturer on "Pastoral Theology," at the Berkeley Divinity School, Middletown, Connecticut.

Bishop Littlejohn is prominently connected with the management of the Domestic Missions of the Episcopal Church. While pastor of the Church of the Holy Trinity, he became a director of the "Society for the Increase of the Ministry," a member of the Executive Committee of the "Sunday School Union and Church Book Society," and president of the "Homes of the Aged and Orphan on the Church Charity Foundation."

He has been for many years a contributor to the "American Quarterly Church Review." Among the articles most favorably known to the public are reviews of Sir James Stephens' "Lectures on the History of France;" Cousin's "History of Modern Philosophy;" the "Character and Writings of Coleridge;" the "Poems of George Herbert," and the "Alt-Catholic Movement in Europe." Many of his occasional sermons, Episcopal charges, and convention addresses have also been published.

"Dr. Littlejohn is one of the ablest preachers in the Episcopal pulpit. His sermons are thorough in a masterly exposition of the theme, and equally able in polish and effectiveness of diction. On all subjects of learned research, on points of church doctrine, and in moral discussions, he shows equal ability, and reaches the conviction of his hearers by the one road of intelligent, eloquent reasoning. His style of delivery is subdued, and exceedingly well disciplined. His words, rather than himself, are impassioned. Whatever strength his thoughts may gain from their mode of delivery, never arises from anything like excitement in himself, but altogether from a distinct, firm voice, and a manner which is almost that of authority. His sentences rise into the grander conception of logic, and they grow touching with pious seriousness; he startles the minds and stirs the hearts of others, but he remains calm and emotionless himself. Avoiding every tendency to render the preacher conspicuous, he only seeks to make the sermon a fitting part of man's intelligent worship in the house of the ever-living God."

Bishop Littlejohn is above the medium height, and has a well-formed, stately figure. His head is large, with a strikingly intellectual forehead, and features remarkably expressive.

CHARLES HENRY DAVIS.

REAR-ADMIRAL CHARLES H. DAVIS, LL.D., a naval officer and mathematician, was born in Boston, Massachusetts, January 16, 1807. He was the son of Daniel Davis, an able lawyer of Massachusetts, who was Solicitor-General of that State for more than thirty years.

In 1823 Charles Henry Davis entered the navy as midshipman; and for more than half a century his name continued on the rolls of the Navy Department. His first nautical service was performed in the frigate "United States," which was attached to the Pacific Squadron. After serving there and on the sloops-of-war "Boston" and "Erie," he passed his examination and joined the "Ontario," on the West India Station, in 1830. Not long afterwards he was promoted to a Lieutenancy.

In 1844 he was assigned to duty on the Coast Survey, and remained in that position until 1849. In 1846-9, while surveying the waters about Nantucket, he discovered the "New South Shoal" and several smaller shoals, directly in the track of ships sailing between New York and Europe and of coasting vessels from Boston. These discoveries were thought to account for a number of before unexplained accidents and wrecks.

During and after his connection with the Coast Survey, he was engaged in examining the state of the harbors of Boston, New York, Charleston, &c. These investigations induced him to study the laws of tidal action. The result of these investigations was his "Memoir upon the Geological Action of the Tidal and other Currents of the Ocean," and "The Law of Deposit of the Flood Tide." He also published a translation of Gauss's "Theoria Motus Corporum Cœlestium," made some shorter translations, and was the author of articles on mathematical astronomy and geodesy. He originated the "American Nautical Almanac," and superintended its publication from 1849 to 1856, when he was ordered to active service in the Pacific in command of the sloop-of-war "St. Mary."

After the commencement of the Civil War, he was made a Captain, and assigned to the flag-ship "Wabash." At the battle of Port Royal, in which he was Fleet-Captain under Du Pont, he distinguished himself by unusual discretion and courage.

In November, 1861, the "Stone Fleet" sailed from Boston for Charleston harbor, where it arrived about the middle of December, under the command of Captain Davis. This fleet was composed of old hulks of whaling vessels, freighted with granite. Its purpose was the effectual obstruction of the harbor of Charleston. This precise and exceedingly difficult operation Captain Davis successfully accomplished.

His services in this regard being duly appreciated, he was given command of the naval flotilla on the Mississippi River, taking the place of the gallant Foote, who was unable to retain his position in consequence of having been severely wounded. That he might regularly assume this command, he was promoted to the rank of Flag-Officer, in May, 1862. On the 11th of that month he repulsed an attack by the Confederate flotilla. Then he in turn made an attack, and succeeded, on June 6th, in capturing or destroying all but one of the enemy's vessels. This action was immediately followed by the surrender of Memphis. He then joined Admiral Farragut, and was actively engaged in the naval operations below Vicksburg, where he displayed great skill and energy. In July he was appointed a Commodore. Together with General Curtis, he operated in the Yazoo River, with complete success, in the following August. During 1863 and 1864 he was most of the time in active service at various naval stations.

When Acting Rear-Admiral Porter returned from the lower Mississippi, Commodore Davis was detached from his command, and ordered to Washington as Chief of the Bureau of Navigation. He remained at that post until April, 1865, when he assumed charge of the National Observatory. After a few years' service in that capacity, the Rear-Admiral—he having attained that rank in February, 1863, being second on the list—was ordered to the command of the Navy Yard at Norfolk, Virginia. In 1873 he was appointed Superintendent of the United States Naval Academy at Annapolis. This post he held at the time of his death, which occurred in that city on the 18th of February, 1877.

Admiral Davis unquestionably took rank with the most thoroughly scientific naval officers of the United States. He was rapid and agile in his movements, an accomplished gentleman, an agreeable social companion, and a brave commander.

SERRANUS CLINTON HASTINGS.

SERRANUS CLINTON HASTINGS was born in Jefferson County, New York, November 22, 1814. His grandfather emigrated from England to Rhode Island early in the seventeenth century, and afterwards settled in New York. Robert Collins Hastings, his father, was a well-educated and intelligent mechanic. He was a warm friend and supporter of De Witt Clinton, after whom he named his son. While that son, the eldest of his little family, was quite a young lad, the father died, leaving his wife and five children destitute.

Young Hastings' boyhood was a continued struggle for the necessities of life and for the means of obtaining an education. He was enabled to study for six years at Gouverneur Academy, and at the age of twenty he became principal of the Norwich Academy in Chenango County, New York, where he introduced the Hamiltonian system of instruction in the languages, the analytical system of mathematics, and improvements in other branches of education. After teaching one year, he studied law for a few months with Charles Thorpe, of Norwich.

In 1834 he went to Lawrenceburg, Indiana, where he completed his legal studies, and in 1836, during the Presidential contest, edited a Democratic paper, "The Indiana Signal." In December, 1836, he went to Terre Haute, Indiana, and in January, 1837, removed to Burlington, in the Black Hawk Purchase, now the State of Iowa. He established himself on the western bank of the Mississippi River, where the city of Muscatine now stands. Having been admitted to the bar, he began the practice of law. Shortly after he was appointed Justice of the Peace by Governor Dodge, of Wisconsin, with a jurisdiction of ninety miles, but had only one case brought before him.

Iowa, successively a part of Missouri, Michigan, and Wisconsin Territories, was created a separate Territory in June, 1838, and was admitted to the Union in December, 1846. The first permanent settlement in the State was made in 1833, four years before Mr. Hastings went there. From the date of the first Legislature assembled under the Territorial government to the admission into the Union as a State, he was a member of the body, either in the House or Council. At one time he was President of the Council. As a member of the Judiciary Committee he reported the celebrated statute, known in Iowa as the "Blue Book." He was prominent in the "Missouri War," occasioned by Missouri officials attempting to collect taxes within the limits of Iowa. After the difficulties were adjusted, Mr. Hastings was appointed one of the Governor's staff, with the rank of Major of Militia.

In 1846 he was elected a Representative of Iowa in the twenty-ninth Congress, where, with one exception, he was the youngest member of the House. In January, 1848, he was appointed Chief-Justice of the Supreme Court of Iowa, which position he resigned in a little over a year.

The discovery of gold in 1848 was the turning-point in the fortunes of California. One of the many who soon became identified with that important State was Mr. Hastings. He settled in Benicia in 1849. Not long after he was unanimously elected, by the Legislature, Chief-Justice of the Supreme Court, and served for two years. In 1851 he received the Democratic nomination for Attorney-General of California. He was elected, and at the end of his two years' term of office retired from public life. The ability he displayed while in public office, both in Iowa and California, proved his native strength of mind and character. Through these years he never neglected his own business affairs. His great wealth and influential position are the result of his perseverance and practical capability.

Mr. Hastings has spent much of his leisure time in travelling extensively in the United States and in Europe. In 1869 he was the guest of the late William H. Seward in his tour of observation through Oregon, Washington, and Alaska. In August, 1870, Governor Seward commenced his "Travels Around the World." During his brief stay in San Francisco he was the guest of Mr. Hastings, who had made the great commercial metropolis of the Pacific his place of residence.

Mr. Hastings is of active nervous temperament, possesses genial manners, and an agreeable presence, is tall in stature, of powerful frame, and has great physical endurance. He is a good Latin scholar, is blessed with large and liberal views, extended information, and fine conversational powers.

RUTHERFORD BIRCHARD HAYES.

RUTHERFORD B. HAYES, the nineteenth President of the United States of America, was born in Delaware, Ohio, October 4, 1822. He is of Scotch descent. His ancestor, George Hayes, came from Scotland in 1680, and settled in Connecticut. Rutherford Hayes, the fifth in descent from him, emigrated from Vermont to Ohio, four or five years before the birth of the son now holding the office of President.

Rutherford B. Hayes received his education at Kenyon College, from which he was graduated in 1842, at the head of his class. Immediately after his graduation he began the study of law in the office of a prominent practitioner of Columbus, Ohio; but soon afterwards determined upon a course of study in the Harvard Law School at Cambridge, Massachusetts. He was graduated from that institute in 1845, and was admitted to the Ohio bar during the same year. For some time he practised professionally at Fremont, and then at Cincinnati, to which city he removed in 1849. He became a member of the Cincinnati Literary Club, among the members of which were many young men who subsequently became prominent and influential. In 1852 he married Miss Lucy Ware Webb, a daughter of Dr. James Webb, of Chillicothe.

Mr. Hayes' law practice increased with the advance of time, and he gradually became favorably known in Ohio. His connection with the "Simmons Murder Case" attracted attention throughout the State. In 1856 he was nominated for the office of Judge of the Court of Common Pleas, but did not accept the nomination. In 1858 the office of City Solicitor for Cincinnati was made vacant by the death of Judge Hart, and the City Council elected Mr. Hayes to serve throughout the unexpired term. He discharged his duties so acceptably that at the next election, in 1861, he was chosen a candidate for the same office. But although he received five hundred votes ahead of his ticket, he was not elected.

Soon after the commencement of the Civil War, Mr. Hayes was appointed Major of the Twenty-third Ohio Volunteers. The regiment went to West Virginia, and was placed on garrison duty. Through the summer months of 1861, Major Hayes served on General Rosecrans' staff as Judge-Advocate. In October he became Lieutenant-Colonel, and commanded the regiment throughout the ensuing winter. At the battle of South Mountain, in September, 1862, he received a wound in the arm, which disabled him for active duty for several weeks. Soon after his recovery he was appointed Colonel of the Twenty-third Regiment. From December, 1862, to the fall of 1864, he commanded the First Brigade of the celebrated Kanawha Division, to which the Twenty-third Regiment was attached. His next promotion was to the rank of Brigadier-General "for gallant and meritorious service in the battles of Winchester, Fisher's Hill, and Cedar Creek," to take rank from October 19, 1864; and he was also brevetted Major-General "for gallant and distinguished services during the campaigns of 1864 in West Virginia, and particularly in the battles of Fisher's Hill and Cedar Creek." During the war he was wounded four times, and four horses were shot under him.

In 1864 General Hayes was elected a Representative in Congress, for the session of 1865–'66. While in the House of Representatives he made no speeches, but was active in the discharge of his official duties. He served upon the Committee of Private Land Claims, and as Chairman of the Committee on the Library. He was also a delegate to the Philadelphia "Loyalists' Convention" of 1866, and to the "Soldiers' Convention," held at Pittsburg. In 1866 he was re-elected to Congress, but resigned in the summer of 1867, and was subsequently elected Governor of Ohio. In 1869 he was re-elected. As chief executive of the State, Governor Hayes won the respect of all classes. In 1872 he again became a candidate for Representative in Congress, but was not elected. In 1875 he became for the third time Governor of Ohio.

Not the least important event of the centennial year was its memorable Presidential campaign. The National Republican Convention, held at Cincinnati, in June, 1876, nominated Governor Hayes as the Republican candidate for the Presidency. He was elected in the following November, and in March, 1877, entered upon his duties as Chief Magistrate of the United States.

Sam¹ Osgood

SAMUEL OSGOOD.

The Osgoods, now numerous in America, seem to have sprung from three of the name, Christopher, John, and William, who came early, in Old Colony times, from the County of Hampshire, England. They were probably kinsmen, and the first two perhaps brothers. The name, apparently, came to England with the Danes, and appeared conspicuously there even previous to the Norman Conquest. Christopher Osgood was the progenitor of that branch of the family to which Dr. Samuel Osgood belongs, in the seventh generation, and he came over in the "Mary and John" to Massachusetts in 1634. Dr. Osgood's parents were Thomas Osgood and Hannah Stevens, his wife, who went from their home-farm in Andover, Mass., soon after their marriage, in 1792, to Charlestown, Mass., where Samuel, their twelfth child, was born August 30, 1812. He was prepared for Harvard University by Dr. Willard Parker, was graduated there in 1832, completed his theological course at the Cambridge Divinity School in 1835, preached in the West and South for nearly two years, took charge of the Unitarian Church in Nashua, N. H. in 1837, was called to the Westminster Church, Providence, R. I., in 1842, and in 1849 went to the pulpit of the Church of the Messiah, New York, as the successor of Dr. Orville Dewey, where he remained twenty years, to the year 1869. He then resigned his position, and sought relief from his long and continuous ministry in a voyage to Europe and in foreign travel. Upon his return he entered the ministry of the Protestant Episcopal Church, which had been for some years congenial to his tastes, and which, as illustrated by its leading writers and preachers and in its home influences, finally won his love and convictions. This was the church of his ancestors, and in his opinion the most comprehensive and edifying of religious organizations. Since that time Dr. Osgood has continued to occupy the pulpit at intervals and to maintain various professional relations, but he has not assumed the entire charge of a parish.

SAMUEL OSGOOD.

Dr. Osgood married, May 24, 1843, Ellen Haswell Murdock, of Boston, who, on the mother's side, is grand-niece to Susanna Haswell, better known as Mrs. Rowson, the author of "Charlotte Temple" and several other poetical and educational works which obtained celebrity in their day. Dr. Osgood received the degree of A.M. at Harvard in 1835, and S.T.D. in 1857. In 1872 Hobart College conferred upon him the degree of LL.D.

Dr. Osgood has accomplished a considerable amount of literary work since he entered the profession in 1835. During his temporary service in Cincinnati and Louisville, in 1836-'37, he assisted Dr. James Freeman Clarke in editing the "Western Messenger." In Nashua, N. H., he wrote for the "Christian Examiner." With C. J. Fox he edited the "New Hampshire Book," and published translations from De Wette and other authors. While in Providence he wrote mostly for the "Christian Examiner," the "North American Review," and other periodicals, and delivered several careful courses of lectures that were afterwards published. In New York, while Minister of the Church of the Messiah, he published "Studies in Christian Biography," 1851; "God with Men," 1853; "The Hearth Stone," 1854; "Mile Stones," 1855; "Student Life," 1860; "American Leaves," 1867; "Christian Worship," in conjunction with Rev. Dr. Farley, 1862; also "Book of Vespers," the same year. He also published many sermons and addresses, among them an Oration before the Alumni of Harvard University, 1860; Discourse before the Harvard Divinity School, 1863; and the Anniversary Discourse before the New York Historical Society (1866), of which he was for ten years Domestic Corresponding Secretary.

Since his withdrawal from the Unitarian denomination, he has written much for the press, published quite a number of discourses and addresses, and brought out new and enlarged editions of "The Hearth Stone" (1875) and "Mile Stones" (1876). His letters from Europe were continued nearly a year in the "New York Evening Post," and he has published memoirs of F. D. Maurice, Thomas Crawford, James Walker, William C. Bryant, Evert A. Duyckinck; and also centennial articles upon Coleridge, Spinoza, Rousseau, Voltaire, and others. His principal contribution to the "Church Congress," of which he has been an active member, was an "Essay on the Ethics of Art," at Boston, 1876; and he is at present pursuing studies in preparation for a work upon a kindred subject, "The Renaissance in America."

ULYSSES SIMPSON GRANT.

ULYSSES S. GRANT, the eighteenth President of the United States of America, was born at Point Pleasant, Clermont County, Ohio, April 27, 1822. In 1839 he entered the military academy at West Point. At the end of the usual four years' course he was graduated,—standing in rank about the middle of his class,—and immediately entered the United States Army as brevet Second Lieutenant of Infantry. Not long after his graduation the Mexican War broke out. He joined General Taylor on the Rio Grande in 1846, and was in the battles of Palo Alto, Resaca de la Palma, and Monterey. He was subsequently with the army of General Scott before Vera Cruz, and participated in every engagement that occurred between that city and Mexico. For meritorious conduct at Molino del Rey and Chapultepec, he received brevets of First Lieutenant and Captain. After the war he was appointed Captain while on duty with his regiment in Oregon. In 1854 he resigned his commission and settled in the vicinity of St. Louis, Missouri, where he was for several years engaged in farming. In 1859 he removed to Galena, Illinois, and entered into business as a manufacturer of leather. Upon the breaking out of the Civil War, Ulysses S. Grant was among the first to offer his services to his country. Governor Yates appointed him Colonel of the Twenty-First Regiment of Illinois Volunteers, and he was at once engaged in active service in Missouri. In August, 1861, he became Brigadier-General of Volunteers, his commission bearing the date of the previous May, and he was assigned to the command at Cairo. He at once occupied Paducah, Kentucky, and late in the following autumn broke up the Confederate camp at Belmont, opposite Columbus. In February, 1862, he commanded in an attack on Fort Donelson. The Fort was surrendered on the 16th. General Buckner, the Commander, wrote to General Grant offering capitulation. Grant replied that no terms would be accepted except an "unconditional surrender," and that he "proposed to move immediately upon their works." These expressions have been frequently popularly quoted, and U. S. Grant has been often said to signify *Unconditional Surrender Grant*.

ULYSSES SIMPSON GRANT.

For his conduct at the siege and capture of this post he was at once commissioned Major-General of Volunteers, his rank to date from February 16, 1862. He advanced to Pittsburg Landing, where, while awaiting the arrival of Buell with reinforcements, he was attacked on the morning of April 6th, by Generals Johnston and Beauregard. After an obstinately contested battle, Grant was driven back toward the river, where he made a successful stand. Reinforcements arrived during the night, the battle was renewed the next day, and the Confederates were repulsed. In September, 1862, he was appointed to the chief command in West Tennessee. He led his forces in person at Iuka on the 19th of that month, and at the second battle of Corinth. In the Vicksburg campaign, from November, 1862, to July, 1863, he gained the highest reputation as a commander. He was appointed Major-General of the United States Army, July 4, 1863, the date of the capture of Vicksburg. He received the thanks of Congress, and was presented with a gold medal in honor of his victory over Bragg's Army at Lookout Mountain and Missionary Ridge, November 24 and 25.

The possession of Chattanooga, which they soon occupied, gave entire control of East Tennessee to the Union forces. In March, 1864, the hero of Vicksburg and Chattanooga was made Lieutenant-General, and on the 17th assumed command of the armies of the United States. He at once commenced the siege of Richmond, which continued until the spring of 1865, when, on the 9th of April, General Lee surrendered the Confederate forces to General Grant.

After the close of the war General Grant made Washington his headquarters, and in July, 1866, was commissioned General of the United States Army, the rank having been created for him. From August, 1867, to February, 1868, he was Secretary of War *ad interim.*

The National Republican Convention which met in May, 1868, nominated General Grant for the office of President of the United States. He was elected the following fall, and was inaugurated March 4, 1869. He was re-elected for the term 1873-7. Under his administration the country rapidly recovered from the effects of the late war. One of the memorable events of this epoch in our national history was the opening in 1869 of the Pacific Railroad, now known as the Central Pacific, to distinguish it from other roads crossing the continent. "The Fifteenth Amendment" was formally announced as a part of the constitution in March, 1870.

After General Grant's retirement from official life he travelled extensively abroad, and everywhere received distinguished attention.

William Cullen Bryant.

WILLIAM CULLEN BRYANT.

WILLIAM CULLEN BRYANT, the poet, orator, scholar, and journalist, was born in Cummington, Massachusetts, November 3, 1794.

He began to write verses at the age of nine years, and at ten composed a little poem for a public school, which was published in a country newspaper. When he was but thirteen years old, a collection of his poems was printed in Boston, entitled "The Embargo; or Sketches of the Times—A Satire." The next year a second edition was printed, together with the "Spanish Revolution," and it was necessary to prefix a certificate of their authorship to satisfy the incredulity of the public. At Williams College he was distinguished by his fondness for the classics. Before the completion of the regular course of study, he left college to prosecute the study of the law. He was admitted to the bar, and was engaged in the practice of his profession at Plainfield for one year, and afterwards for nine years at Great Barrington. In 1816 his celebrated poem, "Thanatopsis," which was written when he was but eighteen years old, appeared. His efforts were not confined to verse; he contributed a number of prose articles to the "North American Review," and in 1821 he delivered a didactic poem on "The Ages," before the Phi Beta Kappa Society of Harvard College. The same year several of his poems were collected into a volume and published at Cambridge.

In 1825 Mr. Bryant removed to New York City, and was engaged as editor of the "New York Review," to which he contributed both prose and verse. In 1826 he became associated with "The New York Evening Post," one of the oldest and most influential newspapers in the city. It was founded in 1801, by William Coleman, an eminent Federalist. During Mr. Bryant's connection of more than half a century with the paper, he reversed its politics, making it decidedly Democratic in opinion. From 1827 to 1830 he was connected with R. C. Sands and G. C. Verplanck in the editorship of a successful annual called "The Talisman." For the "Tales of the Glauber Spa" he wrote "The Skeleton's Cave" and "Medfield." In 1832 the first general collection of his poems appeared in New York; and Washington Irving, then in England, caused it to be reprinted there and by a eulogistic preface secured the author a European reputation. Since that time Mr. Bryant's poems have been collected at intervals in new editions. He visited Europe in 1834, again in 1845 and 1849, and his journal while there, and in the Southern States, the West Indies, and the Holy Land, was published in a volume entitled "Letters of a Traveler." In 1857-8 he made a fourth visit to Europe, which was described in a series of letters to the "Evening Post," and published in 1859 as "Letters from Spain and Other Countries." He devoted several years to translating the "Iliad" and "Odyssey" of Homer into English blank verse. He took part also in writing a "History of the United States." It has been said of his productions, "they contain no superfluous word or empty phrase, but are marked throughout by pure, manly, and straightforward English." Some of his orations and addresses have been collected in a volume. A work entitled "Picturesque America," superbly illustrated, appeared under his editorship.

Mr. Bryant, on several occasions, was called upon to speak in public on the life and services of his eminent countrymen. He pronounced the funeral oration of Thomas Cole, the painter, and delivered a discourse on the life and writings of James Fenimore Cooper. At the dedication of the Central Park statue to S. F. B. Morse, in 1871, he made an address on his life and achievements. The last public demonstration in which he participated was the unveiling of the Mazzini bust in Central Park, May 29, 1878. At the close of the ceremonies, which were in the open air and under the warm sunshine, he accepted an invitation to rest himself at the residence of General James Grant Wilson. As, after a long walk, he reached the top of the steps leading to the front entrance of his friend's house, he was attacked by syncope, and fell backwards, striking his head heavily. He was taken to his home, where he died on the 12th of June, in the eighty-fourth year of his age. He has been justly called the father of American poetry, because he wrote the earliest classical American poem, although his friend the poet Richard H. Dana was an older man.

The tributes of respect to his memory came from all parts of the country and from all classes of people, and the press of Europe joined in the testimonial. The funeral sermon was preached by the Rev. Dr. Bellows, and commemorative orations were given by Hon. John Bigelow, the Rev. Dr. Osgood, and Mr. George Wm. Curtis.

HENRY BOWEN ANTHONY.

HENRY B. ANTHONY, United States Senator, was born in Coventry, Rhode Island, April 1, 1815. His ancestors were among the oldest inhabitants of that state, their Anglo-Saxon blood and Quaker principles at once indicating their origin and their character. Receiving a classical education, Mr. Anthony was graduated at Brown University in 1833. In 1838 he assumed the editorial charge of "The Providence Journal," and soon gave evidence in its columns of his good sense, his practical energy, and his varied learning, spiced with a refined humor that enlisted the attention of readers. He was a decided, outspoken partisan, yet his editorial articles were free from that spirit of acrimony which so often disfigures American journalism, and he was a fair exponent of the principles of the glorious old Whig party, ever directing the fluctuating current of public opinion into safe channels. A stalwart champion of Rhode Island, of her sons and daughters, of her traditions and her institutions, it was not strange that the young editor became a general favorite in his native State.

In 1849 Mr. Anthony was elected Governor of the State of Rhode Island, and he was re-elected in 1850, but he declined being a candidate for a third term. Retiring from the gubernatorial chair he again devoted his whole time to his editorial labors until 1859, when the Republicans of Rhode Island elected him United States Senator, to succeed Hon. Philip Allen, a Democrat. He took his seat in the Senate on the fifth of December, 1859, and has since continuously occupied it, having been successively re-elected in 1863, in 1871, and in 1877. He is now the Pater Senatus.

Gov. Anthony's editorial labors qualified him for his senatorial duties. A man may be born a senator as a man may be born a poet, but it is almost as rare an event, yet there can be no better training for the high position than to have successfully conducted for years—as Gov. Anthony had—a leading journal, and to have acquired the art of harmonizing opinionated contributors and ambitious politicians. He was soon valued as an industrious worker on committees which shape legislation, and he has always been a favorite in the diplomatic and home-circles of Washington, wit and learning embellishing his brilliant conversation, while his social virtues give to his life a rare beauty.

At the outbreak of the great Rebellion Gov. Anthony took a decided stand in defence of the Union. Although a conservative, and by birth and by education a lover of peace, he faced the secession movement with unflinching firmness, and advocated its unconditional defeat. The sagacity which prompted, the decision which nerved, and the resolutions which supported him are stamped upon the congressional annals of the war for the suppression of the rebellion; and the soldiers and sailors of Rhode Island will ever cherish their recollections of his patriotic generosity.

Gov. Anthony was chairman of the Senate Committee on Public Printing during the eighteen years of Republican ascendency in that body, from 1861 to 1879, during which time great improvements were made, under his careful direction in the execution of the work, while its cost was greatly diminished. He has also been, since 1863, a prominent member of the Committee on Naval Affairs, and he has served on several other committees. Displaying rare abilities as a parliamentarian and as a presiding officer, and deservedly popular among his associates in the Senate, Gov. Anthony was elected in March, 1863, president pro tempore of that body, and was re-elected in March, 1871, serving for four years.

Gov. Anthony is not a frequent speaker, but when he does address the Senate he is always listened to with attention. His eloquence is practical and sensible, unadorned with worthless verbal embroidery, yet throughout its solid senatorial sentences there is a classic grace that charms the ear, while his dignified presence, pleasing manner, and pleasant voice aid in gratifying the audience. He has been especially happy in his remarks in the Senate when funereal honors have been paid to deceased Members of Congress whose virtues, public services, and acquirements he has commemorated in undefiled English. These funereal discourses are not merely scholarly productions, but the heartfelt expressions of a generous colleague, vitalized by sympathy, yet not enervated by sentimentality—pearls and golden beads strung upon a black thread. And the crowning characteristic of Gov. Anthony's long public career, as Editor, as Governor, and as Senator, is, that he has invariably regarded with kindly tolerance those who have been his most earnest political opponents, thus carrying out the maxim of the faith of his fathers: "Always treat your enemy of to-day as if he might become your friend of to-morrow."

Bayard Taylor,

BAYARD TAYLOR.

BAYARD TAYLOR, the celebrated American traveller and author, was born in Kennett Square, a village in Chester County, Pennsylvania, January 11, 1825. He was the son of a farmer, descended from a Quaker family, who were among the first emigrants to that State, and associated with William Penn. He received a common school education, and at the age of seventeen became an apprentice in a printing-office in Westchester. He employed his few leisure hours in studying, and in writing verses, in which he was cordially encouraged by such invaluable friends and counsellors as N. P. Willis, Parke Godwin, and Horace Greeley. In 1844 he collected his poems into a volume entitled "Ximena." Having conceived the purpose of a pedestrian tour in Europe, he secured employment as contributor during his absence to some of the leading American newspapers, and commenced his adventurous journey in 1844. After about two years of travel and study he returned to his native country, and published an account of his experiences in "Views Afoot," an agreeably written volume.

In 1848 Mr. Taylor published his "Rhymes of Travel." In the same year he became permanently connected with the "New York Tribune." The following year he visited California, returning by way of Mexico in 1850. His "Eldorado; or Adventures in the Path of Empire," describes this visit. His "Book of Romances, Lyrics, and Songs" appeared in 1851, in which year he commenced a protracted tour in the Old World, including a journey of four thousand miles in the interior of Africa. He also travelled in both Europe and Asia. While in China he was attached to the American Legation for two months, and then accompanied Commodore Perry's squadron to Japan. He reached New York near the close of the year 1853, having accomplished more than fifty thousand miles of travel. The descriptive letters contributed to the columns of the "New York Tribune" during his journey, furnished materials for several of the books of travel he subsequently published. In 1858 his narrative of a journey performed in the winter of 1856-7, entitled, "Northern Travel, Summer and Winter Pictures of Sweden, Denmark, and Lapland," appeared. He also published "Travels in Greece and Russia, with an Excursion to Crete."

In 1862 Mr. Taylor was appointed Secretary of the American Legation at St. Petersburg, and for some time acted as Chargé d'Affaires. He retired from the office in 1863, and the ensuing year he published "Hannah Thurston: A Story of American Life." This was followed in 1865 by "John Godfrey's Fortunes, related by Himself." About the same time his "Poems of the Orient," "Poems of Home and Travel," "The Poet's Journal," and a general collection of his "Poetical Works," were published. His other principal works are "The Picture of St. John," a poem of artist life; "The Ballad of Abraham Lincoln;" "The Masque of the Gods;" "Lars: A Pastoral of Norway," dedicated to the poet Whittier; "Colorado, a Summer Trip;" "Frithiof's Saga;" "Byways of Europe;" and a translation of "Faust," which has been accepted as the best reproduction of Goethe in the English tongue. In 1872 he assumed the editorship of the "Illustrated Library of Travel, Exploration, and Adventure," a series of duodecimo volumes containing a connected compilation of what is known of various lands and races. He also contributed largely to many magazines, periodicals, and journals, and delivered numerous lectures.

In April, 1878, Mr. Taylor, having been appointed Minister Plenipotentiary near the Court of the German Empire, sailed from the port of New York amidst such demonstrations of popular favor as few other men have received under similar circumstances. His appointment was as welcome to the German people as it was to his appreciative countrymen. For many years it had been his chief literary ambition to write a comprehensive biography of Goethe, and he anticipated that his position as American Minister at Berlin would afford very desirable facilities for investigating the personal history of this German celebrity. But his contemplated task was destined not to be completed. His death occurred at Berlin on the 19th of December, 1878.

The tidings of Mr. Taylor's death were received with universal sorrow in his native country. Unusual honors were paid to the memory of the deceased Minister, not only by American poets, scientists, and men of letters, but by many distinguished foreigners, who were numbered among his warm personal friends and admirers. His remains were received in New York, March 13th, 1879, with appropriate public respect and distinction, and were subsequently conveyed to their final resting-place near his home at Cedar-croft, Pennsylvania.

ROBERT BONNER.

ROBERT BONNER, the editor and proprietor of the "New York Ledger," was born within twelve miles of the city of Londonderry, Ireland, April 28, 1824, and descends from Scotch Presbyterian ancestry.

An uncle in this country wrote to the family, inviting Mr. Bonner's older brother to emigrate to America. The invitation was gravely received by the young man, and he half declined its acceptance, when some one said jocosely, "Let the old man go with him." The "old man" (as Robert was then called in his father's family) was a stripling of fifteen years. He turned the joke into sober earnest, and in 1839 arrived in Hartford, Connecticut, where he found his uncle a prosperous farmer and large land-owner within the city limits.

Soon after his arrival in the New World, young Bonner entered the office of the "Hartford Courant" as an apprentice to the printer's trade. He quickly learned this business, and before long could set up more type in a day than any other man in the State. In 1844 he left the office of the "Hartford Courant" with a thorough knowledge of presswork, and went directly to New York, in which city he still resides.

After some delay Mr. Bonner obtained employment in connection with the "Evening Mirror," which was edited by the poets N. P. Willis and George P. Morris. In this new situation Mr. Bonner soon gave proof of his literary taste and ability, by contributing to the "Hartford Courant"—at first with a nom-de-plume—brief sketches of noteworthy incidents in the daily life of New York. The way thus opened, he soon became the New York correspondent of newspapers published in Albany, Washington, and Boston.

Mr. Bonner next became engaged in the office of the "Merchants' Ledger." After a short time, during which he was employed in the advertising department, he hired the type of the "Ledger," and not only printed that paper for the proprietor, but two other weeklies. When the owner decided to dispose of his interest in the "Merchants'

Ledger," which was at that time not a prominent paper, Mr. Bonner purchased it. Under his able management the name was changed to that of the "New York Ledger," and it gradually advanced to the high position it now occupies. Soon after it came into his possession he resolved "to graft the 'Ledger' on a literary basis." He succeeded in securing many prominent and popular contributors to the columns of his paper. Among them were "Fanny Fern" (Mrs. James Parton), and many leading writers of this and other countries. Mr. Everett, in his valuable contributions to the "Ledger," which were afterward published as "The Mount Vernon Papers," thus referred to Mr. Bonner and his enterprise: "It may be mentioned as the most extraordinary, the most creditable, and, as an example to others, the most salutary feature of Mr. Bonner's course, that in the entire progress of this great enterprise, and in its present management, he has never signed or endorsed a note of hand, nor borrowed a dollar; and that in every part of his immense establishment, Sunday is a day of rest."

By his industry and sagacity Mr. Bonner has acquired a large fortune, a goodly proportion of which he devotes to the benefit of his fellow-men. Large sums have been given to aid in erecting a gymnasium for the students of Princeton College, to those sufferers by the Chicago fire who were connected with the newspaper business, and to numerous churches. In addition to all this, thousands of dollars have been expended in charitable gifts, known to none but donor and recipients.

Mr. Bonner indulges his own wishes in one respect. His ambition is to own the best trotting horses in the world, and in this aim he is successful. His stables contain the finest collection of thoroughbreds in the United States, if not in the world. They are never allowed to take part in public races, but are solely for the pleasure of the owner, who visits them each day and drives them himself.

"Mr. Bonner is five feet seven and a half inches in height, and weighs one hundred and seventy-five pounds. He is broad-shouldered, broad-chested, straight, firm, and well proportioned. He has a resolute, determined step, and walks with an air of decision. He has a remarkably large head, and a massive forehead. Brilliant hazel eyes, well set, sparkle with every word he utters. His hair is dark brown, and of fine quality. His full beard is sandy, darkly shaded. His skin is fair. The nose is keen and pointed. The mouth is small, with two rows of as fine white and evenly set teeth as were ever seen. His manner is cheerful, frank and open, and his address free and courteous."

Yours affectionately
J Summerfield

JOHN SUMMERFIELD.

WILLIAM SUMMERFIELD, the father of the celebrated preacher, was a native of Devonshire, England. After filling various situations of trust in England and Ireland, he emigrated with his family to the State of New York, where he died in 1825.

John Summerfield was born in Preston, Lancashire, England, January 31, 1798, and almost from infancy exhibited remarkable precocity of intellect. At the age of five years he was sent to school, and before twelve months had elapsed was considered the best reader in the entire school. When but six years old he attended a school about twenty miles distant from his home. He was next placed under the instruction of Mr. Berry, of Preston, who pronounced him the best grammarian of his age with whom he was acquainted.

Like most boys young Summerfield was fond of play, and his unusual aptitude for rapidly committing his lessons to memory afforded ample time for recreation. His father determined to spare no expense in educating a son of such promise, and accordingly sent him to a celebrated seminary at Fairfield, an extensive Moravian establishment about four miles from Manchester, England. After five years of study at this institution, his father's pecuniary misfortunes recalled him to his home, where he at once made himself practically useful in various ways. In the year 1810, he opened a night-school. Among the pupils who presented themselves were young men nearly twice his own age. The school continued in successful operation until the removal of the teacher to Liverpool, in the following year. In that city he became clerk in a mercantile establishment, being principally employed in conducting the French correspondence of the house.

After the removal of the family to Dublin in 1812, young Mr. Summerfield's conduct for several years occasioned great distress and anxiety to his friends. He fell into evil companionship and very irregular habits of life. Generous and credulous, he could never refuse assistance to an unfortunate friend. His imprudence in this respect often involved him in serious difficulties. At one time he was in prison in Liverpool for seven months in consequence of accepting bills for the accommodation of business acquaintances. Throughout four years of idleness he at times experienced the deepest remorse and penitence. Abandoning his disreputable courses at the age of nineteen years, he joined the Wesleyan Methodists.

After Mr. Summerfield became a member of the Methodist society he frequently delivered exhortations at prayer-meetings and elsewhere, and expounded given passages of Scripture at religious conversation meetings. His first regular public preaching was in Dublin, in April, 1818. He rapidly attained popularity, and preached almost incessantly in Cork and its vicinity. Suffering seriously from ill-health, he passed the summer of 1820 in England with a hope that change of air and scene would be beneficial. He returned in August and continued to occupy various pulpits in Cork and its vicinity until the middle of the following October, when he became alarmingly ill. In a few weeks, however, he so far recovered as to attempt a sea-voyage by the advice of his physicians. His father had long contemplated removing to America, and his son's continued ill-health finally decided him to cross the Atlantic with his family. They arrived in New York in March, 1821. For the four succeeding years young Mr. Summerfield was employed in the itinerant ministry of the Methodist Episcopal Church of the United States.

Soon after his arrival he was received as a preacher by the New York Conference, and at once became unprecedentedly popular in the city of New York. His eloquence attracted crowds of auditors, among whom were persons of all sects and creeds. Ministers of almost every denomination invited him to preach for them. In 1822 he visited Philadelphia, Baltimore, and Washington, in each of which cities he preached to immense congregations.

Mr. Summerfield's health becoming still more feeble, he went to Paris in December, 1822. After visiting England, he returned to New York City in April, 1824, not much improved in health; but still continued to travel and to preach with unabated success, almost to the time of his death, which occurred June 13, 1825.

Mr. Summerfield was one of the founders of the American Tract Society, and was a member of its Publishing Committee. He was also President of the Young Men's Missionary Society.

The degree of A. M. was bestowed upon him in 1822, by Princeton College, New Jersey.

PETER STUYVESANT.

New York, "The Empire State," ranks first in the American Union in commerce, internal improvements, population, and wealth. The first permanent settlements made in the State consisted of two small trading forts erected on the Hudson River by emigrants from Holland, and a few dwellings built on Manhattan Island, where New York City, then called New Amsterdam, now stands. This colony received the name of "Nieuw Nederlandt," or New Netherlands. In 1625 the Dutch West India Company sent out Peter Minuit, or Minnewit, as the first director or governor of New Netherlands. He returned to Holland in 1632, and the following year he was succeeded by Wouter Van Twiller. After his removal from office in 1637, William Kieft was appointed in his place. Kieft was recalled in 1645, and was followed by Peter Stuyvesant, the last and ablest of the four Dutch Governors, who entered upon his duties in 1647.

Peter Stuyvesant was the son of a clergyman in Friesland, Holland, where he was born in 1602. He was educated for the ministry, but eventually decided to enter the army, where he rose to distinction. He served in the West Indian war of that period. Subsequently the West Indian Company appointed him director or governor of the Island of Curaçoa. In 1644 he led an unsuccessful expedition against the Portuguese Island of St. Martin, and lost a leg in the engagement. Returning to Holland for surgical aid, he soon after received the appointment of governor of New Netherlands, and arrived there in May, 1647.

When Governor Stuyvesant arrived in New York he found public affairs in confusion, in consequence of the mismanagement of the previous administration, and at once commenced vigorous measures for restoring order. He was a strict and vigilant officer, and an aristocrat by birth and education, while the sentiments of the people in general were strongly Democratic.

In the spring of 1638, Peter Minuit, the ex-director of New Netherlands, brought over a number of Swedes to establish a colony in the New World. They made their first settlement in Delaware, on a tract of land lying near Wilmington, which they called New Sweden. Governor Stuyvesant exerted all his energies in preventing what he considered encroachments upon the territory under his command. He laid claim to all the lands and streams from Cape Henlopen to Cape Cod. The Puritans of New England had also encroached upon the possessions of their Dutch neighbors. Through the promptness and skilful diplomacy of Governor Stuyvesant, the difficulties arising from these conflicting claims were amicably settled, and a boundary line was agreed upon with Connecticut. Most of the other disputed boundaries between these two nationalities were also adjusted to their mutual satisfaction. Heading an armed force, Governor Stuyvesant now marched against the Swedes, and in 1655 captured the Swedish fort, Casimir (afterwards known as New Castle), in Delaware Bay. The Swedes thus intimidated submitted to the warlike Hollander, and for some time continued under the authority of the Governor of New Netherlands.

In 1664 Charles II., of England, ignoring the claims of the Dutch to New Netherlands, conferred a grant upon his brother, the Duke of York and Albany, which included all the mainland of New England, beginning at St. Croix and extending to the Connecticut and Hudson rivers, "together with the said river called Hudson's River, and all the lands from the west side of Connecticut River, to the east side of Delaware Bay." There were in the Dutch colony some English emigrants who persistently demanded rights and privileges of self-government similar to those enjoyed by the people of Connecticut. Their bearing and influence was a source of great annoyance to Governor Stuyvesant, who was strongly opposed to Democratic institutions. At this juncture an English fleet came to anchor in the harbor of New Netherlands, and demanded the surrender of the town in the name of the Duke of York. "Stout-hearted old Peter pleaded with his council to fight. But in vain. They rather liked the idea of English rule. The surrender was signed, and at last the reluctant governor attached his name. In September, 1664, the English flag floated over Manhattan Island. The colony was named New York in honor of the proprietor." After Governor Stuyvesant had thus been deprived of his command, he went to Holland to report to his government, and subsequently returned to the city of New York, where he spent the remainder of his life in retirement on his farm. He died in August, 1682. His remains were deposited within the walls of the Second Reformed Dutch Church of New York City, which was erected on the ground now occupied by St. Mark's Church.

CORNELIUS VANDERBILT.

Commodore Cornelius Vanderbilt, the "Railroad King," was born on Staten Island, May 27, 1794. His ancestors for three generations had lived and died in the same neighborhood. They came originally from Holland, and in the pages of an old Dutch Bible, still preserved, is written the record of the family for over two hundred years.

Cornelius Vanderbilt spent the days of his childhood in Port Richmond, his native town. An active boy, fond of a stirring out-door life, books and learning did not receive much attention from him. His studies, in fact, were confined to reading, writing, and the rudiments of arithmetic. He worked on his father's farm, sailed on his market boat, which made constant trips to New York City, and, in one way and another, found plenty to occupy his time. During his boyhood, his father procured several boats, in which he used to carry passengers to and fro between Staten Island and the great metropolis, thus establishing a general system of ferriage. When about fifteen years old, Cornelius thought it was time to commence business on his own account. Consulting his mother, who did not seem very much in favor of the plan, she at last reluctantly promised him one hundred dollars, if he would plough, harrow, and plant an eight-acre lot within a certain number of days. Cornelius, nothing daunted, accepted the terms, and at once began the seemingly impossible feat. Letting some boy friends into the secret, they willingly agreed to help him, and at the specified time the task was completed. Scarcely was his reward received, when he invested it in a craft smaller than the average used for the purpose, but more manageable and much faster. The young ferryman was successful from the first. His boat was patronized by passengers, and he occasionally carried freight. During the war of 1812, he frequently transported sick and wounded soldiers from the forts to the city. As business increased, he built other boats. The introduction of steamboats into New York and New Jersey waters soon started rival lines. One of the first gentlemen to own one of these new vessels was Mr. Thomas Gibbons. In 1817 he engaged Cornelius Vanderbilt as captain of a small steamer, at a salary of one thousand dollars a year.

CORNELIUS VANDERBILT.

He spent twelve years in the service of Mr. Gibbons, and in that time mastered the system of steam navigation. For the next twenty years he continued in the same business on his own account. During that period he built a very large number of steamboats, and established steamboat lines on the Hudson, Long Island Sound, and elsewhere.

In 1851, having previously obtained from the Government of Nicaragua a charter for a Ship Canal and Transit Company, the "Commodore," as the public styled him, opened a new line from New York to California by the way of Nicaragua. Under his management, the route became a favorite one, and the price of passage was reduced one-half. He constructed very many first-class steamers for both the Atlantic and Pacific sides of this line. In 1853 he sold his steamers to the Transit Company. In 1856 he was chosen the President of the Company. He built the steamship "North Star," furnished it, took his family and made the tour of Europe, for a pleasure trip. This was the first steamer fitted with a beam engine that ever attempted to cross the Atlantic. In 1855 he established an Independent line between New York and Havre. Among the new steamships built for this line, was the "Vanderbilt," which cost eight hundred thousand dollars. In 1862, when the United States navy needed large and immediate additions, the Commodore made this magnificent vessel a present to the Government, for which Congress passed a resolution of thanks.

In 1863, Mr. Vanderbilt was chosen President of the New York & Harlem Railroad Company. He had been connected with this road (the first running from New York City) for several years, first as stockholder, and then as a director. About this time he disposed of the last of his steamships, and afterward gave his undivided attention to railroad matters. In 1865, he was elected President of the Hudson River Railroad Company, while holding the same office on the Harlem. Before long, he obtained a controlling interest in the Central Company, a rival line, and in 1868 was elected its President. The next year the Central and Hudson River Railroads were consolidated into one company, called the New York Central and Hudson River Railroad—of which Commodore Vanderbilt was President.

Mr. Vanderbilt died in his home in New York City, January 4, 1877. During his eighty-two years of life he had amassed immense wealth. At the time of his death his property was calculated at seventy millions of dollars, and may possibly have reached one hundred millions.

JOHN CALDWELL CALHOUN.

JOHN C. CALHOUN, LL.D., one of the most eminent statesmen of his time, was born in Abbeville District, South Carolina, March 18, 1782. His father, Patrick Calhoun, a native of Ireland, and a man of great energy and resolution, commanded a company for frontier defence in the Revolutionary War. His mother, Martha Caldwell, was of Scotch-Irish descent. Even in boyhood he gave promise of future eminence. Grave, thoughtful, and fond of reading, he devoted himself to substantial works, to the entire exclusion of light literature. Though naturally an ardent and earnest student, he received little systematic education until he had almost reached years of maturity. After a short time spent in preparation, he entered the junior class at Yale College, in 1802, and was graduated with high honors in 1804. While there, he won the high admiration and esteem of Dr. Dwight, then president of the institution. Upon the completion of his college course he commenced the study of law, was admitted to the bar in 1807, and at once commenced legal practice in his native district.

As early as 1808 Mr. Calhoun entered public life, his career extending over a period of more than forty years. He was elected to a seat in the State Legislature, and after serving two sessions with ability and distinction, was chosen to represent his district in Congress. Immediately after taking his seat he was appointed by the Speaker, Henry Clay, one of the Committee on Foreign Affairs. He was greatly instrumental in procuring the declaration of war with England in 1812, and was an able supporter of President Madison's administration. His speech on the Loan Bill, in 1814, was one of his most eloquent and patriotic efforts. As chairman of the committee on national currency, he, in 1816, introduced the bill to establish a National Bank. After six years of important service in the House of Representatives, he was called to the Cabinet of President Monroe, as Secretary of War. He held that office throughout Monroe's administration, and by his admirable management thoroughly systematized the affairs of the Department. In 1825 he was elected to the Vice-Presidency of the administration of John Quincy Adams, at the termination of which he continued in the same office with President Jackson. In 1831 he resigned the Vice-Presidency to become the successor, in the United States Senate, of Robert Y. Haynes, who vacated his place to become Governor of South Carolina. Mr. Calhoun took his seat as the acknowledged champion of Nullification. One of his most powerful oratorial efforts was made against the celebrated Force Bill. "As the presiding officer of the Senate he was punctual, methodical, and accurate, and had a high regard for the dignity of the body which he endeavored to preserve and maintain. His views of the tariff, his opinions in regard to slavery, and the many and exciting questions connected with it, are well known. He shaped the course and moulded the opinions of the people of his own State, and of some other Southern States, upon all these questions. Amid all the strifes of party politics, there always existed between him and his political opponents a great degree of personal kindness." Webster, one of these antagonists in debate, but a warm friend, said of him: "He had the indisputable basis of all high character, unspotted integrity, and honor unimpeached." That distinguished statesman delivered an eloquent tribute to his memory when his death was announced in the Senate. At the end of the term he retired to private life. In 1843 he succeeded Mr. Upshur as Secretary of State, and upon the close of Mr. Tyler's administration he was returned to the Senate. His last speech was on the slavery question, but his health was so infirm that it was read by a friend, March 4, 1850. He died on the 31st of that month. From 1811, when he entered Congress, until his death, he was rarely absent from Washington.

"In person he was tall and slender. His features were harsh and angular in their outlines, presenting a combination of the Greek and the Roman. His countenance, when at rest, indicated abstraction or a preoccupied air, and a stranger on approaching him could scarcely avoid an emotion of fear, yet he could not utter a single word before the fire of genius blazed from his eyes and illuminated his expressive features. His individuality was stamped upon his acute and intelligent face, and the lines of character and thought were clearly and strongly defined. He was easy in his manners, affable, and dignified. He was kind, generous, charitable, honest, frank, and faithful to his friends, but somewhat inclined to be unforgiving toward his enemies. He was attached to his principles and prejudices with equal tenacity; and when he had adopted an opinion, so strong was his reliance upon the correctness of his own judgment that he often doubted the wisdom and sincerity of those who disagreed with him."

Andrew Jackson

ANDREW JACKSON.

ANDREW JACKSON, the seventh President of the United States, was a remarkable man, who possessed "great virtues and great defects." He was of Scotch-Irish descent, and was born in Waxham, South Carolina, March 15, 1767. His father died before he was born, and his mother was very poor. His boyhood was devoted to athletic and out-of-door sports. He was not fond of study, and the opportunities offered him were not improved as they should have been. About the age of fourteen he enlisted in the Continental Army of the revolution, in which his two brothers were killed. He was with Sumter when defeated at Hanging Rock, in 1780. In 1781 he was captured by the British, and for refusing to clean the commander's boots received two wounds from a sword and was sent to prison, where he contracted small-pox. His mother effected his exchange, but died shortly afterward. Left entirely destitute, young Jackson tried various employments, indulging in the meantime in the wild sports and dissipation of the day. He finally settled down to the study of law, and was admitted to practice in Western North Carolina, now Tennessee, in 1786. When that part of the country became a territory, in 1790, President Washington appointed him Attorney of the United States for the new district. He was one of the delegates to the convention at Knoxville for forming the State Constitution at Tennessee, and when it was admitted to the Union, in 1796, he was chosen its first representative in Congress. He made the journey of eight hundred miles to Philadelphia, where the sessions of Congress were then held, on horseback. In 1797 he was chosen a United States Senator to fill a vacancy.

After his return to Tennessee, in 1798, Mr. Jackson was elected a judge of the Supreme Court of that State. This office he held for six years. His decisions, though when written were ill-spelt and ungrammatical, are said to have been generally right in the main. About the time he was elected judge, he was chosen major general of the Tennessee militia, and held the office until called to the same rank in the United States service in May, 1814, during the second war with Great Britain. Soon after the opening of hostilities he joined the army, and first distinguished himself in the battles with the Creek Indians, who were allies of the British, at Talladega, in November, 1813, at the Emuckfau in January, 1814, and at Horse-shoe Bend in March, 1814. In the summer of that year General Jackson was commissioned to treat with the subdued tribes and to establish military posts in their country. By the signal victory he obtained over the British at New Orleans, in January, 1815, and by his active and vigorous measures for the defence of that city, he established his reputation as a general. In 1817 and 1818 he successfully conducted the Seminole War in Florida, and soon after resigned his commission in the army. In 1821, President Monroe appointed him Governor of Florida, which office he resigned in a few months. In 1823 he was elected, by the Legislature of Tennessee, to a seat in the United States Senate. In 1824 he was one of the four candidates for the Presidency, but was not successful.

In 1828 the "Hero of New Orleans" was elected President of the United States, by the Democratic party. Upon his inauguration in the following March, he at once surrounded himself by his political friends, thus establishing the now popular principle of rotation in office. During the first year of his administration there were nearly seven hundred removals from office, not including subordinate clerks. During the preceding forty years there had been but sixty-four. He was re-elected in 1832. The principal events of his memorable administration were the difficulties with France about the paying of the indemnity, the suppression of the nullification movement in South Carolina, the war with the Seminole Indians, and the United States Bank troubles. With the masses of the people he was the most popular President, with the exception of Washington and Lincoln, the country has ever had. At the close of his administration he retired to his home, the Hermitage, near Nashville, Tennessee, where he died June 8, 1845.

The life of Andrew Jackson was unusually replete with exciting adventures. He was, in every particular, a remarkable man. His chief intellectual gifts were energy and intuitive judgment. He possessed great firmness and decision of character. He had an instinctive horror of debt. From early boyhood his hot temper and inflexible will involved him in constant quarrels, and sometimes in personal encounters. Though intense in his prejudices, slow to be convinced, and having many defects of character, "Old Hickory," as he is still called, was admired for his thorough honesty of purpose and sincere patriotism. Soon after his retirement from the presidency he became a Christian, and his subsequent life was consistent with his profession.

HANNIBAL HAMLIN.

HANNIBAL HAMLIN, a prominent United States statesman, was born in Paris, Oxford County, Maine, August 27, 1809. When nearly prepared to enter college the impaired health of an elder brother recalled him from school to assist upon the paternal farm. At the age of eighteen he commenced the study of law under the direction of another brother residing in the eastern part of his native State. Little progress had been made in this respect, however, when the death of his father necessitated young Hannibal's return home to take charge of the farm, and for two succeeding years he continued in this position.

About the time he became of age he spent a year in a printing office as a compositor, and was associated with Mr. Horatio King in the proprietorship of the "Jeffersonian," a paper printed in his native town. He then resumed the study of law, at the end of three years was admitted to the bar, and entered at once on the practice of his profession. On the very day of his admission he gained a case. In April of that year, 1833, he removed to Hampden, near Bangor, where he has since resided. When established in his new location he directly entered upon a large practice, which he continued for fifteen years, during that time frequently delivering political and other addresses.

From 1836 to 1840 Mr. Hamlin was annually elected a member of the Legislature of Maine, and for three of those five years was Speaker of the House of Representatives. He was elected a Representative of his native State to the Twenty-eighth Congress, and was reëlected for the following term. He served on the Committee on Naval Affairs and was Chairman of the Committee on Elections. In 1847 he again became a member of the House of Representatives in the Maine Legislature.

In May, 1848, he was elected to the Senate of the United States for four years, filling a vacancy occasioned by the death of John Fairfield. He was reëlected for the full Senatorial term in July, 1851. All these

JAMES BUELL.

JAMES BUELL, President of the Importers and Traders' National Bank of New York, and also of the United States Life Insurance Company of New York, was born at Glen's Falls, Warren County, New York, March 23, 1820. As long ago as 1630, a William Buell, of Wales, crossed the ocean, and after a short stay in Massachusetts settled in Windsor, Connecticut. The New England families descended from him have had several members prominent in the history of the country. Among them were Major David Buell, the late Rev. Dr. William Buell, of Albany, General Don Carlos Buell, a commander during the late Civil War, and Mrs. Sarah Josepha Hale, the well-known authoress. At the time of her death, which occurred in Philadelphia, in May, 1879, she was about ninety years of age, and had retained her mental faculties to a remarkable degree. In November, 1877, she resigned her position as editress of Godey's "Ladies' Book," which she successfully conducted for fifty years. Her brother, Horatio Buell, a graduate of Dartmouth University, who was for many years a judge at Glen's Falls, was the father of James Buell.

Before Mr. James Buell had reached the age of fifteen years he had lost both his parents. The four following years were spent on the farm of his grandfather. He then entered a dry goods store, in Troy, N. Y. After several years' experience as a clerk, he commenced business for himself in the same city, and for eight years was a successful merchant, acquiring a high reputation for fair dealing and sagacious enterprise. At the expiration of this time he became cashier of the Central Bank of Troy. His connection with this institution lasted five years, when he accepted an invitation to fill a similar position in the Importers and Traders' Bank of New York City. He entered upon his duties in 1857, succeeding Mr. George R. Conover. His diligent labors to promote the interests of the bank were appreciated, and in 1865 he was unanimously elected president in place of Lucius Hopkins, who had then just resigned, after filling the position since the organization of the bank ten years before.

When President Buell was elected the bank possessed a surplus of one hundred and fifty thousand dollars, and the market value of its shares was about eight per cent. above par. Under his management the surplus has increased to more than a million and a half of dollars. During the same period the market value of the stock nearly doubled, while for several years an annual dividend of fourteen per cent. has been paid to the stockholders. A distinctive feature of the institution is its allowance of interest on accounts of banks and bankers. Under this system the deposits have reached the enormous aggregate of eighteen and a half millions of dollars, an amount greatly in excess of that held by any other bank in the United States.

"Probably no one of the many very able financiers at the head of New York bank institutions enjoys a larger reputation throughout the country than Mr. Buell. While in a measure this circumstance is due to the exceptionally good results of his management as a bank president, and to the liberal and extended nature of the relations fostered by him between his own bank and provincial institutions, the high estimation in which he is held at all the money centres is, in a still greater degree, a recognition of his earnest efforts to harmonize and systematize the banking institutions of the Union, and to establish the national finance upon a permanent and secure policy. In the furtherance of his well-considered scheme of gradual and sure redemption, Mr. Buell's public address and written papers upon the subject of currency have added largely to the literature of banking, winning for him a professional credit hardly less pronounced than that awarded to the more pretentious treatises of Gilbart and Goshen in England."

In 1874 the Committee on Banking and Currency of Congress invited Mr. Buell to visit Washington and unfold his views of a proper remedial policy before that body. His theory of national credit and currency impressed the committee and the public, and was emphatically endorsed by the ablest political economists of the country. In 1875 the measure known as the Sherman bill was prepared. One clause of which was the virtual adoption of Mr. Buell's plan for the increase of national bank circulation. In July of that year the first meeting of the American Bankers' Association was held at Saratoga, and Mr. Buell was placed at the head of the Committee on Resolutions. Before the adjournment of the convention, a committee of permanent organization was formed with Mr. Buell as chairman, and he was afterward made President of the Executive Council.

In the latter part of 1875, Mr. Buell was appointed President of the United States Life Insurance Company of New York.

JOHN ADAMS DIX.

MAJOR-GENERAL JOHN A. DIX was born in Boscawen, New Hampshire, July 24, 1798. He received his early education at the academies at Salisbury and Exeter, and spent a year in a French seminary in Montreal, Canada. In 1812 he was appointed a cadet in the Military Academy at West Point. Before he commenced his professional studies the war with Great Britain began, and he joined the army on the frontier as an ensign. Within a few months he was promoted to a third, and then to a second lieutenancy, and also served as acting adjutant of a battalion. In 1819 he was appointed an aide-de-camp of General Brown, and in 1825 he was promoted to a captaincy in the Third Artillery, but, his health becoming impaired, he obtained leave of absence and travelled in Europe and the West Indies. In 1828 he retired from the army and established himself in Cooperstown, New York, in the practice of law. He soon became an active and influential member of the Democratic party. In 1831 Governor Throop appointed him Adjutant-General, a post of duty which he filled with honor to himself and advantage to the militia of the State. In 1833 he became Secretary of State of New York. While occupying that position he was a member of the Canal Board and one of the Commissioners of the State Canal Fund. He was also superintendent of common schools, and a Regent of the University of the State of New York.

In 1842 Mr. Dix became a member of the State Assembly, and took a leading part in its proceedings. After making another visit abroad, he was elected to the United States Senate to fill the vacancy caused by the election of Silas Wright as Governor of the State of New York. His term extended from January, 1845, to March, 1849. In that body he bore a prominent part in the discussions on the annexation of Texas, the Mexican war, the Oregon boundary dispute, and the question of slavery in the Territories, upon which he expressed the views of the Free Soil Democrats. That party made him its candidate for Governor of New York in 1848, but he was not elected. Upon the expiration of his Senatorial term he was succeeded by William H. Seward. He took an active part in promoting the election of Franklin Pierce to the

Presidency in 1852, and about that time declined, in favor of William L. Marcy, an offer of the post of Secretary of State. In 1853 he was made Assistant Treasurer of the United States in the city of New York, but soon resigned.

In 1860 President Buchanan appointed General Dix Postmaster of the city of New York. In January, 1861, he was appointed Secretary of the United States Treasury, and held the office until the 6th of the following March. While serving in this capacity he used the celebrated phrase with which his name will always be associated. Being informed that the commander of the revenue cutter "McClelland," at New Orleans, was about to betray that vessel to the Confederate authorities, he telegraphed to the second officer to depose him, and, if he should resist, to treat him as a mutineer. The despatch concluded: "If any one attempts to haul down the American flag, shoot him on the spot!" After the civil war had fairly commenced, General Dix was made Chairman of the Union Defence Committee, and presided over the memorable meeting of the citizens of New York in Union Square. In May, 1861, he was appointed a major-general of United States volunteers, and was soon after placed in command of the newly created Department of Maryland. In June, 1862, he was transferred to Fortress Monroe, and subsequently held command of the Department of the East.

On the organization of the Pacific Railroad Company, General Dix was elected its President. In 1866 he was a delegate to the National Union Convention held in Philadelphia. In that year he was appointed Naval Officer for the port of New York, but soon after received the appointment of Minister Plenipotentiary to France. After his return home he was a prominent member of the Committee of Seventy. In 1872 he was nominated by the Republican party as Governor of the State of New York, and was elected. This was the last public office he held, but he subsequently took an active part, by speeches or letters, in the discussion of great national issues. He died at his home in New York City, April 21, 1879.

General Dix was the author of "Resources of the City of New York," "Decisions of the Superintendent of Common Schools," "A Winter in Madeira," "A Summer in Spain and Florence," and two volumes of speeches. In 1820 he received the degree of A.M. from Brown University, and that of LL.D. from Geneva College in 1845. His son, Rev. Morgan Dix, D.D., is a prominent clergyman of the Episcopal Church in New York City.

STEPHEN HIGGINSON TYNG, Jun.

The names of Stephen H. Tyng, and Stephen H. Tyng, Jun., are prominent among those of faithful preachers and workers in the Protestant Episcopal Church of the United States. One of these clergymen has devoted the best years of a long life to his sacred calling, the other apparently has still many years of active usefulness before him.

Stephen H. Tyng, D.D., the father of the subject of this sketch, was born in Newburyport, Massachusetts, March 1, 1800, and was graduated at Harvard College. For the two subsequent years he was engaged in mercantile pursuits, and then began the study of theology, which he pursued under the direction of Bishop Griswold. He was ordained a Deacon of the Protestant Episcopal Church at Bristol, Rhode Island, March 4, 1821. He was for two years rector at Georgetown, D. C., and afterwards for six years in Queen Anne's parish, Prince George's County, Maryland. In May, 1829, he removed to Philadelphia, and became rector of St. Paul's Church in that city. In 1833 he was called to the Church of the Epiphany in Philadelphia. The degree of D.D. was conferred upon him by Jefferson College in 1832, and by Harvard in 1851. In 1845 he succeeded Dr. Milnor as rector of St. George's Church, New York City. After a ministry of thirty-three years his impaired health compelled him to retire from the pastorate, which he did in May, 1878, with the title of Rector Emeritus. He was succeeded by his assistant rector, the Rev. Walter W. Williams. Dr. Tyng has been an active worker in Sunday Schools. For many years he preached specially to children every Sunday afternoon. St George's Sunday School under his pastorate raised and disbursed large sums of money. Among the purposes to which these funds were applied were the erection of four religious edifices in Africa, a stone church and school-house in Moravia, and a brick church and school-house in Caldwell, N. Y. They also sufficed for building, and furnished two chapels in New York City, and for large contributions to different missions.

Dr. Tyng's chief publications are his "Lectures on the Law and the Gospel;" "The Israel of God;" "Christ is All;" and "Christian Titles." He has also published "Recollections in Europe;" "The Captive Orphan—Esther, Queen of Persia;" "Forty Years' Experience in Sunday Schools;" "Prayer Book Illustrated by Scripture," in eight volumes; "The Spencers: A Story of Home Influence;" "Walking with God;" and a Memorial of his eldest son, Dudley Atkins Tyng, D.D., who was, like his father and brother, a clergyman of the Protestant Episcopal Church, and who died in 1858. For several years Dr. Tyng edited the "Episcopal Recorder" and the "Protestant Churchman."

Stephen H. Tyng, D.D., Jun., was born in Philadelphia, June 28, 1839. He was graduated at Williams College in 1858, and studied at the Episcopal Theological Seminary, in Fairfax County, Virginia. While pursuing his professional studies he had charge of a mission church in Georgetown, D. C. The commencement of the Civil War obliged him to leave Virginia before the completion of the prescribed course at the Theological Seminary. He was ordained Deacon at St. George's Church, New York City, May 8, 1861, and was his father's assistant until May, 1862. He was ordained Priest at Poughkeepsie, N. Y., September 11, 1863. Young Dr. Tyng was rector of the Church of the Mediator, New York City, for two years, and then organized a new parish, which was known as the Church of the Holy Trinity. An appropriate building was erected on the corner of Forty-second Street and Madison Avenue, and was consecrated in 1865. Early in 1873 the old church was torn down, and on Trinity Sunday, June 8, 1873, the corner-stone of the present edifice was laid on the same site. The congregation soon became numerous and influential. They support several mission churches in different parts of the city, and also maintain a college, or "House of the Evangelists," for the education of young men for the city mission work. There is a dispensary connected with the church, where each day two physicians gratuitously give advice and medicine. Several beds in St. Luke's Hospital are also endowed by this church.

In 1864 Dr. Tyng accompanied the Twelfth Regiment of New York to Harrisburg, as chaplain.

In 1872 he received the degree of D.D. from Williams College. He is the editor of the "Working Church," a weekly journal. He is a zealous and patient worker, an industrious scholar, an accomplished elocutionist and an eloquent preacher.

CARL SCHURZ.

CARL SCHURZ, who has been for several years prominent in the politics of the United States, was born on the second of March, 1829, at Liblar, a village near Cologne, Germany, where his father was a schoolteacher. After pursuing the usual course of study at the gymnasium at Cologne, he entered the University of Bonn. The outbreak of the revolution of 1848 interrupted the studies of young Schurz, who at once joined the band of "Unity and Liberty" collected around Professor Gottfried Kinkel, of Bonn, one of the best known poets of his day. The Constitutional Assembly of Germany completed a constitution for the country, but the great powers of Germany and several of the rulers of the small principalities refused to recognize it. Southwestern Germany flew to arms in defence of the new constitution, which was designed to secure the privileges demanded by the people, and supporters from other parts of Germany joined in the revolt—among them Kinkel and Schurz. The latter entered the army, and at Rastadt these friends were both taken prisoners. Schurz soon escaped, and eventually succeeded in liberating Kinkel from the fortress of Spandau. Schurz then went to Paris, where he became a correspondent for German journals, and subsequently to London, in which city he was a teacher until July, 1852, when he decided to emigrate to America.

Upon his arrival in America, Mr. Schurz established himself in Philadelphia, where he remained three years, and then settled on a farm in Watertown, Wisconsin. From the time he crossed the ocean, he devoted himself to studying the politics and language of the country he had resolved to make his permanent home. The Republican party had then just been organized, and he at once became an ardent member. In the presidential campaign of 1856 he was recognized as an orator in the German language. In 1858, when Stephen A. Douglas and Abraham Lincoln were contesting the United States senatorship, he delivered his first speech in the English language. It was published and widely circulated. Mr. Schurz next commenced the practice of law at Milwaukee, Wisconsin, and engaged in a lecturing tour in the winter of 1859-'60. In 1860 he was a member of the Nominating Convention at Chicago, and exerted his influence for the nomination of Mr. Seward. In recognition of his services the convention made him a member of the National Republican Committee. In this position he was largely influential in determining that portion of the platform relating to citizens of foreign origin. During the canvas which followed, he spoke effectively throughout the Northern States.

Upon the outbreak of the civil war Mr. Schurz proposed to enter the Union Army, but, soon after Mr. Lincoln's inauguration, was appointed Minister to Spain by the new President. He returned to the United States in January, 1862, resigned his office as minister, and again offered his services to the government as a soldier. They were accepted, and President Lincoln appointed him brigadier-general of volunteers in April, 1862, and as such he participated in the battles fought during that year by the forces commanded by Generals Fremont and Pope. He was afterward at the head of a division in the corps of General Sigel, in which position he distinguished himself at the second battle of Bull Run. In March, 1863, he was made a major-general, and fought at Chancellorsville and Gettysburg.

In 1864 he was active in the campaign for the re-election of President Lincoln, and, after the close of the war, in 1865, he was sent by President Johnson to investigate and report on the condition of the Southern States, especially upon the condition of the Freedman's Bureau.

In the winter of 1865-'66, he was the chief Washington correspondent of the "New York Tribune." In 1866 he became editor of a Republican paper in Detroit, Michigan, but soon after exchanged this position for that of one of the proprietors and editors of the "Westliche Post," a German Republican paper published in St. Louis. He took a leading part in the Chicago convention of 1868, of which he was temporary chairman. In the winter of 1868 the Legislature of Missouri elected Mr. Schurz to the Senate of the United States—the highest position attainable by a citizen of foreign birth. In the presidential campaign of 1872 he favored the Liberal Republicans, and advocated the election of Horace Greeley in numerous stump speeches, delivered in nearly all parts of the country. In the Senate he assumed a prominent part in all financial debates, and advocated the resumption of specie payments. He left the Senate at the expiration of his term, in 1875, and advocated the election of Rutherford B. Hayes for the office of President of the United States in the national campaign of 1876.

In 1877 he was appointed Secretary of the Interior, in the Cabinet of President Hayes.

WILLIAM HENRY SEWARD.

This eminent statesman was born May 16, 1801, in the town of Florida, Orange County, New York. In after years he endowed a Seminary in his native town, which was named after him, the "Seward Institute." He was the son of Dr. Samuel S. Seward. At the age of fifteen he entered Union College, Schenectady, and was graduated with distinction in 1820. He studied law under John Duer, John Anthon, and Ogden Hoffman, and was admitted to the bar in 1822. In 1823 he selected Auburn, N. Y., as his place of residence, and commenced the practice of law in association with Judge Elijah Miller, whose daughter he married in 1824. In 1828 he was president of a State Convention of young men favoring the re-election of John Quincy Adams. In 1830 he was elected a member of the Senate of New York. For more than forty years from the date of his election to the Senate of his native State, Mr. Seward was prominent, not only in the politics of New York, but of the entire Union. In 1832 he made an able speech in favor of the United States Bank. In 1833, while travelling in Europe, he sent home a series of descriptive letters, which were afterward published in the "Albany Evening Journal." In 1834 he was the unsuccessful candidate of the Whig party for Governor of New York, but was again nominated for that office in 1838, and elected. He was re-elected in 1840. While in the State Senate, and also when Governor of New York, he supported the policy of internal improvement, advocated the abolition of imprisonment for debt, reform in the courts of law and chancery, the extension of education, and other liberal measures. In 1842 Mr. Seward actively resumed his profession, and practised extensively, chiefly in the United States courts. He warmly supported Henry Clay for President in 1844, and General Taylor for the same office in 1848. He was opposed to the annexation of Texas. In 1849 he was elected United States Senator from New York. He was re-elected in 1855, and held that position until he became Secretary of State under Abraham Lincoln. He was distinguished throughout his Senatorial terms by his firm resistance to the extension of the slave power. In March, 1850, he made a speech in favor of the admission of California into the Union. He opposed the Compromise of 1850, and the Fugitive Slave Law. He opposed the Native American party, and was one of the leading founders of the Republican party. In 1859 he went to Europe for the second time, and visited Egypt and the Holy Land. He was a prominent candidate for the nomination for the Presidency in the Republican Convention of 1860. Lincoln being selected as the candidate of that party, Mr. Seward advocated his election, in a series of speeches, during an extended tour. He was called to Mr. Lincoln's cabinet when he became President, and continued to hold the position of Secretary of State until 1869, and exhibited much ability in relation to foreign policy during the Civil War. Among the leading subjects of his diplomacy were the liberation of Mason and Slidell, and the French invasion of Mexico in 1862.

In the early spring of 1865, Mr. Seward was seriously injured by being thrown from a carriage. While still confined to his bed from the effects of this accident, on the night of President Lincoln's assassination, Lewis Payne, an accomplice of J. Wilkes Booth, entered the room of the invalid and inflicted several severe wounds upon his neck and face.

In 1849 Mr. Seward published the "Life and Public Services of John Quincy Adams." His own life and complete works were published in four volumes, between the years 1853 and 1862. It was through his official agency that Alaska was purchased of Russia in 1867.

Being in feeble health, late in the summer of 1870 the venerable statesman commenced a tour of the world, and was received throughout his entire progress with the most distinguished respect and attention. After his return home he superintended the preparation of a large volume entitled, "William H. Seward's Travels Around the World." He died at Auburn, N. Y., October 10, 1872.

Many touching and impressive tributes were paid to his memory, on the occasion of his obsequies, and in April of the following year a special Memorial Service was held at Albany by the Legislature of New York, when an elaborate and eloquent address was delivered by the Hon. Charles Francis Adams.

It was Mr. Seward's fortune to be opposed, in political opinion, by many of the eminent statesmen of the period. But, although not so remarkably endowed by nature in some respects as were several of his opponents, his singularly elegant and effective rhetoric, and his thorough acquaintance with the fundamental principles of statesmanship and civil law, never failed to triumph in debate, and to be admiringly recognized by all persons of discrimination.

WINFIELD SCOTT HANCOCK.

MAJOR-GENERAL WINFIELD SCOTT HANCOCK was born in Montgomery County, Pennsylvania, February 14, 1824. Having graduated at West Point, June 30, 1844, he was appointed Brevet Second Lieutenant in the Sixth U. S. Infantry, and promoted to Second Lieutenant in the same, June 18, 1846. After two years' service in the Indian Territory, he accompanied his regiment to Mexico, and was conspicuous for gallantry in the actions at the "National Bridge," San Antonio, Churubusco, Molino del Rey, and assault and capture of the City of Mexico. He was brevetted First Lieutenant, August 20, 1847, for "gallant and meritorious conduct at the battles of Contreras and Churubusco," and was Regimental Quartermaster, until appointed Adjutant of his regiment, October 1, 1849. Promoted to First Lieutenant, January 27, 1853, and Captain and Assistant Quartermaster. U.S.A., November 7, 1855, he served from June, 1855, as Assistant Adjutant-General, Department of the West, Headquarters at St. Louis, Mo. He was in Southern Florida during the last Indian war, 1856, and in Kansas during the "troubles" there in 1857, and with the Utah Expedition in 1858, and then marched to California, where the outbreak of the Rebellion found him on duty at Los Angelos.

Upon being relieved, at his own request, he hastened to Washington, and was appointed by President Lincoln a Brigadier-General of Volunteers, September 23, 1861, and assigned to a brigade of the Army of the Potomac, and was stationed near Lewinsville, Va., during the fall and winter of 1861-2. In March, 1862, he proceeded to the Peninsula with the army, and was engaged in the siege of Yorktown from April 5th until its evacuation, May 4th. On the following day he led the brilliant charge at "Williamsburg," capturing Fort Magruder, several hundred prisoners, and one battle flag. For this gallant service he was specially complimented by General McClellan in his dispatches. His conspicuous services at "Golding's Farm," June 27, 1862, "Garnett's Hill," June 28th, "Savage's Station," June 29th, "White Oak Swamp," June 30th, and other battles on the peninsula, led the General-in-Chief to recommend his promotion to Major-General of

Volunteers. During the Maryland campaign of 1862, he was at "Crampton's Pass," and in the battle of Antietam was selected to command the First Division, Second Army Corps, after its commander was mortally wounded. In November, 1862, he was promoted to be Major-General of Volunteers. At the great and decisive battle of "Gettysburg," July 1, 1863, he was (after the fall of Reynolds) directed by General Meade, then commanding the Army of the Potomac, to assume command of all the national forces on the battle-field, First, Third, and Eleventh Corps, and Buford's cavalry. On July 2d and 3d he commanded the left centre of our army, and on the 3d his troops repulsed the grand final assault of Lee, capturing 5,000 prisoners, 30 stand of colors, and many thousand small arms. At the moment of victory he was desperately wounded. It was many months before he could again take the field. Congress, by joint resolution, thanked him "for his gallant, meritorious, and conspicuous share in that great and decisive victory."

Upon his return to active duty in May, 1864, he took part in several successful engagements, and in the famous assault at Spottsylvania, May 12, captured more than 4,000 prisoners, 20 pieces of artillery, 30 stand of colors, and two general officers; but his old wound soon compelled him to obtain leave of absence for a short time. In June he rejoined the army and was engaged in several battles. Promoted to be a Brigadier-General in the Regular Army, he was, in November, 1864, called to Washington to organize a Veteran corps of 50,000 men. He was brevetted a Major-General for gallant and meritorious services at Spottsylvania, and on July 26, 1866, promoted to be a Major-General U.S.A. His subsequent military service was in command of various geographical commands, until called, during reconstruction times, to the command of the important Fifth Military District, with his headquarters at New Orleans. Relieved at his own request, his subsequent duty was in the Northwest until called to command the great Military Division of the Atlantic, with his headquarters at Governor's Island, N. Y.

His administration of affairs in the South during reconstruction, and his subsequent utterances at Chicago during internal revenue complications, and on other occasions, as to the due subordination of the military to the civil authority, taken in connection with his splendid military record, have caused his name to be prominently mentioned in connection with the presidency.

It has fallen to the lot of few men to render such continued and valuable service to his country.

GARRET DORSET WALL.

GARRET D. WALL, a lawyer, soldier, and statesman, was born in Middletown township, Monmouth County, New Jersey, March 10, 1783. His father, James Wall, an officer in the war of the Revolution, died when the son was nine years of age. Thereupon he was adopted by his uncle, Dr. John C. Wall, with whom he resided until the death of the latter in 1798. He then removed to Trenton, and, having previously received a fair academical education, entered at once upon the study of law in the office of General Jonathan Rhea, who at that time was Clerk of the Supreme Court of the State. He was a careful student, and after passing the requisite examination was licensed as an attorney, and at once commenced the practice of his profession at Trenton. In 1807 he was advanced to the grade of counsellor-at-law.

In 1812 Mr. Wall was elected Clerk of the Supreme Court for the term of five years. During his term of office the second war with Great Britain occurred. He volunteered his services in a company of uniformed militia, of which he had been a lieutenant for some years. He was made captain of the Phœnix Infantry Corps, and aided in the protection of the city of New York. Upon the expiration of his term as clerk he resumed the practice of law.

Mr. Wall was Quartermaster-General of New Jersey from 1815 to 1837. In 1820 he became sergeant-at-law. In 1822 he was elected, on a "Union" ticket, to represent Hunterdon County in the lower branch of the State Legislature, in which body he distinguished himself by his thorough knowledge of law. Up to this time he had been an earnest member of the Federalist party, but at length he became a Democrat, and was among the earliest supporters of General Jackson for the Presidency. In 1827 he was elected to the General Assembly, and in 1829 was elected Governor of New Jersey by the Legislature, but declined the office. The same year he was appointed United States District Attorney for the State, which station he held for several years, discharging its duties with ability. In 1834 he was elected, by the State Legislature, a member of the United States Senate, where he served during the last two years of Jackson's second term, and the entire four years of Van Buren's administration. He condemned the measures put forth in favor of rechartering the United States Bank, and one of the most effective speeches he delivered while a Senator was in opposition to the advocates for the continuance of that institution.

Upon the expiration of his Senatorial term he returned to Burlington, which town had been his home since 1828, and recommenced his professional practice. In 1843 his health was greatly impaired by a stroke of paralysis. He partially recovered from the attack, and engaged in several important cases. He earnestly advocated the measures which culminated in the assembling of a Constitutional Convention in 1844, and was deeply interested in the adoption of the new Constitution which had been framed by that body. In 1848 he was made a Judge of the Court of Errors and Appeals, in which position his extensive learning and research enabled him to reach an impartial conclusion on the various legal questions submitted to that body. He was occupying that office at the time of his death, which occurred in Burlington, New Jersey, November 22, 1850.

General Wall, as he was called from having filled the office of Quartermaster-General of the State, was of commanding personal appearance. He was a counsellor and pleader of the highest ability. "As a partisan he was remarkably free from party bitterness, and never allowed his friendships to be sundered, though his political belief might condemn the measures advocated by his most intimate and valued associate. He was an earnest advocate for the cause of education, and took a lively interest in the establishment of Burlington College, and was an active member of the Board of Trustees of that institution. He was eminently distinguished for his hospitality and for his willingness to advise all those who sought his counsel, although reaping no pecuniary benefit from it."

His son, James W. Wall, an able lawyer and politician, was a graduate of Princeton College. His first public position was that of Commissioner of Bankruptcy. In 1850 he was elected Mayor of Burlington, New Jersey. In 1854 he visited Europe, and published a volume entitled "Foreign Etchings; or, Visits to the Old World's Pleasant Places." He is also the author of other works. During the early part of the Civil War he wrote against the administration for interfering with the freedom of the press, and was imprisoned for a few weeks in Fort Lafayette. Upon his release he was enthusiastically welcomed home by his fellow-citizens. He was subsequently elected a member of the United States Senate from New Jersey.

REV^D THOMAS COKE L.L.D.

THOMAS COKE.

Thomas Coke, D.D., LL.D., the first Bishop of the Methodist Church in America, was born at Brecon, South Wales, September 9, 1747. He was educated at Oxford University, and after his graduation was elected mayor of Brecon. In 1775 he received the degree of D.C.L. He soon after took orders, and obtained a curacy at South Petherton. While in the exercise of his ministry he made the acquaintance of Mr. Wesley, an allusion to which, dated August 18, 1776, is found in Mr. Wesley's journal: "I preached at Taunton, and afterward went with Mr. Brown to Kingston; here I found a clergyman, Dr. Coke, late a gentleman commoner at Jesus College, who came twenty miles on purpose to meet me. I had much conversation with him, and a union then began which I trust shall never end."

Dr. Coke's preaching being thought too evangelical, he was dismissed from his curacy. Uniting with the Wesleyan Methodists, he preached to immense congregations on the commons and fields of London. In 1780 he was appointed Superintendent of the London Circuit. He assisted Mr. Wesley in securing a proper deed in chancery that the churches might be legally held and the societies perpetuated. He also restricted the conference to one hundred preachers and their successors forever. In 1782 he was appointed President of the Irish Conference. In 1784 Mr. Wesley, having been strongly urged by the Methodists of America to provide a church organization for them, selected Dr. Coke, and ordained him Bishop for America. Upon his arrival in New York, in November, 1784, he sought an interview with Francis Asbury, the result of which was the calling of a conference or general convention of ministers, at Christmas, for the organization of the church. The preachers assembled at Baltimore, and by a unanimous vote resolved to constitute an independent church, to be called the Methodist Episcopal Church, and elected Dr. Coke and Mr. Asbury as bishops; whereupon Dr. Coke ordained Mr. Asbury as bishop. After travelling through the different conferences in company with Bishop Asbury, he returned to England, in June, 1785, and visited Wales, Scotland, and Ireland. He subsequently made other visits to the

United States, which he had designed to make his home; but upon the death of Mr. Wesley the General Conference in America, at the earnest invitation of his brethren, permitted him to reside in England. While in America he exercised the functions of a bishop in ordaining ministers, but in Europe the close connection of the Methodist Societies with the English Church rendered it improper to do so. For many years he presided annually in the Irish Conference, and frequently over the English Conference.

Dr. Coke was deeply interested in the missionary cause, and was successful in planting the church in many places. The first mission which he established was in the West Indies, in 1786. He was anxious to have missions established among the Indians, and also among the Germans in America. Having inherited some wealth, and having that wealth increased by marriage, he not only supported himself, but spent a large part of his fortune in laboring for missions, in behalf of which he collected subscriptions, sent out missionaries, kept accounts, and made reports until his death. In 1797, during one of his visits to America, the vessel he was in was taken by a privateer, and he was most cruelly treated, being plundered of everything but his books. In 1798 he devised a plan of domestic missions for Ireland, and established a mission in Wales. In 1803 he made his ninth and last visit to America. Upon his return he established a mission in Gibraltar, and a few years later one was established at Sierra Leone, through his influence. In 1813 he proposed to the Wesleyan Conference that he would go personally as a missionary to the Island of Ceylon. The Conference objecting on account of the expense, he furnished $30,000 from his private fortune, and, selecting five missionaries, embarked with them the last of December. After a voyage of four months, and when it wanted but a few days of the time the company expected to land, Dr. Coke retired one night feeling a little unwell, and the next morning, May 2, 1814, he was found dead in his cabin. He was buried at sea.

Dr. Coke was deeply interested in education, and shortly after his arrival in the United States he planned with Mr. Asbury the erection of a college, which was named by the conference after both the bishops, "Cokesbury." He was a voluminous writer. Many of his sermons and addresses on theological and ecclesiastical topics were published. He assisted Henry Moore in preparing a life of Mr. Wesley; published "A Commentary on the Holy Scriptures," "History of the West Indies," "History of the Bible," "Defence of the Doctrine of Justification by Faith," and other works.

JAMES SHIELDS.

The life of General James Shields " reads like a romance—lawyer, judge, senator, farmer, knight-errant, and general." He was a native of Dungannon, County Tyrone, Ireland, where he was born in the year 1810. At the age of sixteen he came to this country, and pursued his studies until 1832, when he went to Illinois and commenced the practice of law at Kaskaskia. In 1836 he was elected a member of the State Legislature, and in 1839 he became Auditor of the State. Four years later he was appointed Judge of the Supreme Court of Illinois, and in 1845, having received from President Polk the appointment of Commissioner of the General Land Office, he removed to Washington.

Upon the breaking out of the Mexican War, Mr. Shields was appointed a Brigadier-General of United States Volunteers, his commission bearing date July 1, 1846. He was present at the siege of Vera Cruz, where he was noted for his gallant conduct. At the battle of Cerro Gordo he was severely wounded, but continued on the field, urging on his men, until a ball, passing through his body and lungs, struck him down. He was carried from the battle-field, and was reported to be so near the point of death that obituary notices appeared in nearly all the papers of the country. For weeks his life was despaired of. The story of his cure is remarkable, and would appear improbable had he not lived for many years after without suffering any inconvenience from the wound. The army surgeons had abandoned hope of a favorable result of their skilful treatment, when a Mexican doctor said he would recover if he would allow him to remove the coagulated blood. Shields told him he might make the attempt, and a fine silk handkerchief was worked in and finally drawn through the wound, removing the extravasated blood, when daylight could be seen through the opening made by the shot. For his gallant and meritorious conduct during the battle where he received his wound he was, in August, 1848, promoted to the rank of brevet Major-General. Before fully recovering he commanded a brigade in the valley of Mexico, consisting of a battalion of marines and regiments composed of New York and South Carolina volunteers. He was also in the battle of Chapultepec, where, being unhorsed, he fought, sword in hand, leading his brigade with a bravery that has made his name remarkable in American history. He was again dangerously wounded, but his vigorous constitution enabled him to rally from the effects of his injury. In July, 1848, the brigade he commanded was disbanded, after performing valorous deeds ending in the capture of the City of Mexico, where they unfurled the first American flag. This closed the war, and General Shields returned to civil life.

In 1848 General Shields was appointed Governor of Oregon, but resigned the office. In 1849 he was elected to a seat in the United States Senate. Owing to some technicality he was refused admission as a Senator, when he promptly resigned the post, and was as promptly re-elected. He returned to Washington, and for his term of six years discharged the duties of a Senator. He had been chosen to the post by the Democrats of Illinois, to the interests of whose party he was devoted. In 1855 he settled on the lands awarded to him for his services in the army, which lands he had selected in the Territory of Minnesota. When that tract became a State he was elected to represent it in Congress, and took his seat after its admission in May, 1858. He served two years in this position, after which he removed to California, and resumed the practice of law.

After the breaking out of the Civil War he was appointed by Congress a Brigadier-General, with a commission dated August, 1861. Upon the death of General Lander he was appointed his successor, his division forming part of the corps of Major-General Banks. He particularly distinguished himself in the Shenandoah Valley, where he met and defeated the famous "Stonewall" Jackson, who was at the head of a large body of soldiers. The day before the battle, March 22, 1862, during the preparatory movements, he was severely wounded. At the battle of Port Republic, in June of the same year, he was defeated by General Jackson. Shortly after he retired to Missouri and became a farmer.

In 1868 General Shields was a candidate for Congress in Kansas City on the Democratic ticket, but was not elected. He resided in Missouri during the remainder of his life. His death occurred June 1, 1879, while visiting friends in Ottumwa, Iowa.

General Shields was of good personal appearance, about five feet eight inches in height, with an eye that was bright and full of life, dark grayish hair, and ruddy complexion.

MATTHEW HALE CARPENTER.

Hon. MATTHEW H. CARPENTER, lawyer and senator, was born in Mooretown, Washington County, Vermont, December 22, 1824. In 1843 he entered the Military Academy at West Point, and though his life as a cadet was satisfactory, he did not complete the full course; but, on account of ill-health, resigned his position in 1845. He soon after entered upon the study of law, in the office and under the instruction of the Hon. Paul Dillingham, of Waterbury, Vermont. He soon became complete master of the learning and theories of his profession, and perfectly qualified for practice at the bar, and was accordingly admitted at Montpelier, Vermont, in the spring of 1847.

Mr. Carpenter immediately entered upon the practice of his profession in the office of Hon. Rufus Choate, of Boston. His association as professional assistant with the great lawyer was of much benefit to the young practitioner, and was one cause of his rapid progress and popularity. Without these advantages, his talents, his manners, and his finished style of oratory would have attracted attention and gained success.

After being admitted to the Supreme Judicial Court of Massachusetts, Mr. Carpenter went to Beloit, Wisconsin, the seat of the well-known institution, Beloit College. In this flourishing young city of the West, he soon secured a large and lucrative practice. Soon after his permanent location in the place, he was elected to the office of District Attorney of Rock County, and held it for two terms with great credit. By the energetic and industrious exercise of his abilities, he soon attained a high rank as a profound lawyer and eloquent advocate. Few lawyers have been engaged in more cases or in those of greater importance. In 1851 he conducted a cause involving the questions of dedication to public use, of the legality of city plats, and of estoppel by deed and *in pais* concerning a public landing on Rock River, in the city of Beloit. "The case came to the Supreme Court of the State when at that time in that court such questions were new, and Mr. Carpenter's brief, reported in full with the opinion of the court, is a masterpiece of legal investigation and learning, and the most elaborate to be found in the reports of that court, passing in review the leading authorities in England and this country on the question involved—over one hundred cited cases." In the remarkable proceeding by *quo warranto* to try the title of the office of Governor of Wisconsin, between the relator Bashford and the incumbent Barstow, argued in the Supreme Court in 1856, Mr. Carpenter was the leading counsel for the respondent. His brief in that case, with an abstract of his argument, were also published, with the opinion of the court in the Reports of Wisconsin. His practice in that State constitutes a large part of its judicial history. For several years he practised in the Supreme Court of the United States. He was retained by Secretary Stanton to argue several important causes growing out of the reconstruction measures of Congress, and involving the constitutional powers of the Government.

Mr. Carpenter had been a sympathizer with the Democratic party, but upon the opening of the Civil War he made one of the first addresses in favor of a vigorous war for the Constitution. In 1869 he was elected a United States Senator from Wisconsin to succeed Mr. Doolittle, and took his seat March 4, 1869. He served as a member of the Committees on the Judiciary, Patents, the Revision of the Laws of the United States, and Privileges and Elections. He bore an able part in the debates of the Senate. His speech in reply to Sumner and Schurz, during the French Arms debate, attracted much attention. It is said to have been more widely circulated than any other public document during the political campaign of 1872; more than one million copies having been distributed from Washington alone. In March, 1873, he was elected President of the Senate *pro tempore*.

Mr. Carpenter, when a candidate for re-election to the Senate, was defeated by Angus Cameron, who was supported by a combination of Republicans, Democrats, and Liberals. Leaving the Senate on the expiration of his term, March 3, 1875, Mr. Carpenter resumed the practice of law at Milwaukee and at Washington, with marked success. When the next election for United States Senator took place in Wisconsin, he was nominated by the Republicans in the place of Timothy O. Howe, and elected; so he resumed his seat in the Senate at the called session, which commenced March 18, 1879.

Mr. Carpenter has gathered one of the largest and best selected libraries of law and miscellaneous literature in the country. He is a shrewd parliamentary leader, an agreeable debater, and a fluent speaker, and possesses a striking and attractive personal appearance, with fine eyes, a good complexion, and thick brown hair silvered by age.

Jonathan Edwards

JONATHAN EDWARDS.

Jonathan Edwards, an American divine and metaphysician, was born at East Windsor, Connecticut, October 5, 1703. His father, Timothy Edwards, a graduate of Harvard University, and the first minister of East Windsor, superintended his preparation for college, and trained him to habits of careful study and analysis. Intellect and piety were developed in him very early. At the age of ten he read, with delight, the essay of Locke on the "Human Understanding." When twelve years old he sent, to a European correspondent of his father, an account of the "wondrous way of the working of the spider" in the forest, whose habits he had watched. A few days before his thirteenth birthday he entered Yale College, and completed the full course with high honors in 1720. For two years after his graduation he remained in New Haven as a student for the ministry, and in the summer of 1722 was licensed to preach. Immediately afterward he was appointed to preach to a small body of Presbyterians in the city of New York. This was before the completion of his twentieth year. About this time he finished a series of seventy resolutions, which were to be the guiding principles of his life. These relate to "the absolute performance of duty without regard to immediate motive or difficulty."

In 1724 the young minister was appointed a tutor in Yale College, where he remained until 1726. In that year he became associated with his grandfather, the Rev. Mr. Stoddard, whom he succeeded three years later in his ministry at the Congregational Church at Northampton. He was ordained on the 15th of February, 1727. For the succeeding twenty-three years he continued a faithful pastor, and devoted his efforts to an awakening of zeal and restoration of strict devotional conduct. His fame as a preacher became widely extended during these years. In June, 1750, he was dismissed by an Ecclesiastical Council for insisting upon a purer and higher standard for admission to the communion. In the next year he was installed minister at Stockbridge, Massachusetts, and missionary to the Indians then in that vicinity.

While at this post he wrote his "Essay on the Freedom of the Will," which metaphysicians have always considered unequalled for close and subtile reasoning. During the six years spent at Stockbridge their limited means were increased by the industry of his wife and daughters, whose delicate handiwork was sent to Boston to be sold. On the death of the Rev. Aaron Burr, his son-in-law, who was President of Princeton College, New Jersey, Mr. Edwards was called to succeed him. He was inaugurated February 16, 1758. The small-pox was then prevalent in the vicinity, and Mr. Edwards was innoculated as a precaution. A fever soon set in, which resulted in death, March 22, 1758. He left a large family of children, one of whom, Jonathan Edwards, became a Doctor of Divinity and President of Union College, Schenectady, New York. His only son, Jonathan W., was a distinguished lawyer of Hartford.

Mr. Edwards was tall of stature and of a slender form. "He had a high, broad, bold forehead, and an eye unusually piercing and luminous; and on his whole countenance, the features of his mind—perspicacity, sincerity, and benevolence—were so strongly impressed, that no one could behold it without at once discovering the clearest indications of great intellectual and moral elevation."

The published writings of Mr. Edwards are voluminous, and form a valuable contribution to religious literature. His works are the "Essay on the Freedom of the Will," "Treatise Concerning the Religious Affections," "Inquiry into the Qualifications for Full Communion in the Church," "Original Sin," "Dissertation Concerning the End for which God Created the World," "True Nature of Christian Virtue," "Thoughts on the Revival of Religion," "History of the Redemption," and "Life of David Brainerd." His writings, with a memoir by Sereno Edwards Dwight, were published in ten volumes, 8vo, in New York. His life has been written by several others.

"In considering the writings of Jonathan Edwards, the first thing to be borne in mind is his unquestioning acceptance of the truth of the Holy Scriptures. The next is, the intensity of his attachment to the system of Calvinism as opposed to that of Arminianism.

"Edwards makes a turning-point in the intellectual, or, as he would have called it, the spiritual history of New England. New England and New Jersey, in the age following him, applied more thought to the subject of religious philosophy and systematic theology than the same amount of population in any other part of the world."

SAMUEL GRISWOLD GOODRICH.

SAMUEL GRISWOLD GOODRICH, under his assumed name of "Peter Parley," ranks among the best known of our authors. He was born at Ridgefield, Connecticut, August 19, 1793. His father, the Rev. Samuel Goodrich, was a clergyman distinguished for simplicity of character, strong common sense, and eloquence.

Mr. S. G. Goodrich was educated in the common schools of his native town. Soon after completing his twenty-first year, he engaged in the business of publishing in Hartford, where he resided for several years. In 1824 he visited Europe, devoting his attention particularly to educational institutions. On his return he established himself as a publisher in Boston, where he commenced an original annual, "The Token." Its contributions and illustrations were the products of American authors and artists. It was noticeable for its encouragement of young and unknown writers. The finest of Nathaniel Hawthorne's "Twice-told Tales" were first published in "The Token," without attracting any special attention. The famous Peter Parley series was commenced about the same time.

Mr. Goodrich published many volumes of historical and geographical school-books. In addition to his labors as a compiler, he was the author of prose and poetical works. His "Fireside Education" was composed in sixty days, while he was discharging his duties as a member of the Massachusetts Senate, and superintending his publishing establishment. His numerous other works were produced with surprising rapidity. In 1837 he published "The Outcast, and other Poems;" and in 1841, "Sketches from a Student's Window;" in 1850 his celebrated work, "History of all Nations." He established "Merry's Museum and Parley's Magazine," a most popular monthly, of which he was editor from 1841 to 1854.

In 1855 Mr. Goodrich was United States Consul at Paris, where he made arrangements for the translation and introduction of his Peter Parley series into France. On his return to America he published a book which will perpetuate his name. It is a species of autobiography, entitled "Recollections of a Lifetime, or Men and Things I have

Seen: in a series of familiar letters to a friend, historical, biographical, anecdotal, and descriptive." "In an easy colloquial narrative the author narrates the experience of his boyhood in his New England home, a simple, at times quaint and humorous, story. Though removed from the present day by only half a century, the manners of Connecticut, in the youth of the writer, present many curious details of a simplicity which has almost passed away. As he proceeds, various New England personages of consequence are brought upon the scene, and we have some valuable notices of the war with England of 1812. The literary men of that time, the Hartford wits, the poets, Percival and Brainerd, are introduced. Then comes the author's first journey to England, and his acquaintance with various celebrities among men of letters. His active literary career at home succeeds, followed by his consulship at Paris, which included the period of the revolution of 1848. In the appendix to this work Mr. Goodrich enumerated the books of which he was the editor or author. The recital of the titles occupies six closely written pages. They are chiefly school-books and the various series of the Peter Parley Tales and Miscellanies. 'I stand before the public,' wrote Mr. Goodrich, 'as the author and editor of about one hundred and seventy volumes—one hundred and sixteen bearing the name of Peter Parley. Of all these over seven millions of volumes have been sold.'"

In the preparation of his books for the young he was assisted by his brother, the Rev. Charles A. Goodrich. His latest production was an "Illustrated Natural History," completed in 1859.

The appearance of Mr. Goodrich was singularly vigorous and youthful for one of his years, and his death in New York City, May 9, 1860, was as unexpected to his friends as it was sudden.

His son, Frank B. Goodrich, is the author of several well-known works. He corresponded from Paris with "The New York Times," under the name of Dick Tinto, for several years; and these letters, entitled "Tri-colored Sketches of Paris," were published in New York in 1854. His other works of note are the "Court of Napoleon, or Society under the First Empire, with Portraits of its Beauties, Wits, and Heroines;" "Man upon the Sea, or a History of Maritime Adventure, Exploration, and Discovery;" "Women of Beauty and Heroism;" "The Tribute Book, a Record of the Munificence, Self-sacrifice, and Patriotism of the American People during the War for the Union;" and "Famous Women, a Portrait Gallery of Female Loveliness, Achievement, and Influence."

www.ingramcontent.com/pod-product-compliance
Lightning Source LLC
Chambersburg PA
CBHW030749230426
43667CB00007B/898